Growing Orchids in South Africa
- A Gardener's Guide
Hendrik Venter

Phalaenopsis Pink Leopard "Petra"

Dendrobium Mousmee "Colleen"

Growing Orchids in South Africa
~ A Gardener's Guide

Hendrik Venter

BRIZA

I would like to dedicate this book to my late parents, Piet and Miemie Venter. Without their support and understanding of a teenage boy wanting to grow orchids, I would not have been the orchid grower that I am today. I also wish to thank my wife Anneen and sons Wiaan and Christian for their love, patience and encouragement during the writing of this book.

Thanks also to my mentors in the orchid world who so generously shared their knowledge and friendship with me over the years - the late Hugh Rogers, the late Dulcie Somers-Vine, Ann Duckworth, Carmen Coll and Hendrelien Peters - and too many others to mention. You know who you are - thank you!

This manuscript was proofread by Mrs Hendrelien Peters, who is a stalwart of the orchid judging world in South Africa. She is also an accomplished artist, and is responsible for the line drawings and sketches used in this book.

Most of the photographs in this book were taken by the author. However, in instances where other photographers have kindly lent the author their slides, photographic accreditation is listed on page 144.

Briza Publications
PO Box 56569
Arcadia
0007
South Africa
www.briza.co.za

Tel: +27 (0) 12 329-3896
Fax: +27 (0) 12 329-4525

First Edition, First Impression 2006

© No part of this book may be reproduced or transmitted in any form or by any electronic or mechanical means, including photocopying and recording, or by any other information storage or retrieval system, without written permission from the publisher.

All rights reserved

ISBN-10: 1-875093-80-X

ISBN-13: 978-1-875093-80-9

Managing editor: Joanita Fourie

Photography: Hendrik Venter

Layout and design: Annalene Rautenbach

Cover design: Annalene Rautenbach

Printed and bound by
TienWah Press (Pte) Ltd, Singapore

Contents

Chapter 1 - Introduction to Orchids and their History   7

Chapter 2 - Basic Botanical Information on Orchids   13

Chapter 3 - General Growing Information   23

Chapter 4 - Orchids by Genus - General Cultural Information   37

Chapter 5 - Recommended Orchids   51

Chapter 6 - Repotting and Dividing your Orchids   115

Chapter 7 - Indigenous Orchids   125

Chapter 8 - Contact Information   135

Recommended Further Reading   139

References   140

Index   141

Photographic Credits   144

Dendrobium Mild Yumi "Dream"

1

Introduction to Orchids and their History

Typical habitat for orchid explorers - Giant's Castle, South Africa

The History of Orchids

Orchids have fascinated people for many centuries, and will no doubt continue to do so for many more. The Chinese were the first people to cultivate orchids, namely certain indigenous *Cymbidium* species, which were grown in fancy containers. The orchids were prized for their charm, beauty and fragrance. They were mostly grown by the nobility.

The big orchid-growing craze where orchids were beginning to be cultivated as a plant family started in England. Commercial growers such as Messrs Veitch and Sander were renowned plant collectors in Victorian times and even earlier. Many famed botanists got to grips with the plants that intrepid explorers and collectors sent home to England from around the globe. Initially, these growers were not all that interested in orchids, in fact, orchids were not widely grown at all. Collectors sent all types of plants to their employers, but these were plants that were better known as commercially viable prospects.

A fortunate incident happened early in the nineteenth century when one of these collectors, William Swanson, shipped a cargo of plants to England, to a grower and plant enthusiast called William Cattley. Swanson had used an unusual plant that he had found in Brazil as packaging material to secure the shipment of plants. The plant itself was not known to him, but Mr Cattley was intrigued by the unusual growth habit of the packaging material, and decided to grow it to see if it would flower. As it happens, this packing material turned out to be *Cattleya labiata*, a species with up to two magnificent large pink/lilac flowers. The genus was eventually named in honour of Mr Cattley. The race to amass the largest collection of the most beautiful and rare orchids was on in earnest.

Professional orchid hunters scoured the globe for new and different species, and it has been recorded that thousands upon thousands of orchid plants were collected in the wild and sent to England by ship. Of course, ideal conditions did not prevail on these ships, as plants were packed in crates and simply shipped without being watered or otherwise cared for. Thousands of plants died on the journey, with only a small percentage making it home alive. Plants that did arrive alive were severely stressed and dehydrated, and were promptly potted up and placed in stove houses, the period's equivalent to the modern greenhouse. English gardeners believed that as the plants came from the tropics, they needed hot and humid conditions. The stove houses were combinations of heavily-painted glass, coal fires and hot brick flues. There was no ventilation, and the bricks were drenched continually with water to produce a steamy atmosphere. In this and many more instances, the plants were subject to mostly unsuitable conditions that did not even remotely resemble their natural habitat. This of course did not help the plants to survive, and even more perished. One nobleman remarked that England had become the "grave of tropical orchids".

This was originally the reason why orchids were so hugely expensive and commanded high prices at auctions held by the growers. The cost of a collection trip was very high, and with the relatively small number of plants that did eventually survive, one can understand why the remaining plants were so sought after. Select plants of good quality and in good condition could attain prices of many thousands of pounds, and in today's terms would simply be too expensive for most people to buy. Because of the high prices of plants at the time, orchids received a reputation as being a rich man's hobby, and only the nobility and the very wealthy had large collections. They often had numerous glasshouses to house their collections, and employed a lot of staff to look after these plants. In many instances, these collections were only grown for pleasure, and as the collections were never sold, one really needed a vast amount of money to fund such a hobby. To this day it is generally assumed that orchids are for the wealthy only, and yet because of modern techniques of propagation and growing, orchid plants are quickly and successfully grown from seed or replicated in laboratories by meristem processes, making them freely available at a fairly nominal cost.

Cattleya labiata

Laeliocattleya Canhamiana - an intergeneric hybrid registered in 1885

The Origin of Orchids

Orchids comprise the largest group of flowering plant species in the world. Approximately 30 000 species are found in the wild, and more are discovered every day. One would think that most have been discovered by now, especially the more spectacular plants, yet surprising discoveries of large and vibrantly coloured flowers are made on a regular basis. As increasingly more previously inaccessible areas are opened by exploration and development, new and interesting species are found regularly. Of course, this holds true for all other plant families, insects and animals.

Tens of thousands of man-made hybrids have resulted due to the curiosity of man, and many of these are registered in a worldwide central database maintained by the Royal Horticultural Society at Kew in England. Orchid hybrids are probably the most accurately recorded of all floral hybrids, and each modern hybrid, due to the registration process, can trace its family tree, even through many generations, back to the original species involved.

Orchids occur throughout the world, from sea level up to the snowline. A vast number of species, mostly warm to intermediate growing, are found in South America in the tropical and subtropical areas such as the Amazon rain forest and surrounding areas. However, many also grow in mountainous regions, and some species, which prefer the colder areas (e.g. *Masdevallia*), are found higher than two thousand metres in the Andes and other montane areas.

Orchids also abound in several countries and islands in the Far East, for example Thailand, Borneo, Sumatra, and the Philippines. They mainly occur in the warmer areas. Orchid growers, especially in South Africa, should not regard this as a problem - warmer-growing plants are those that thrive in temperatures between 18-30°C. This is certainly easy to attain in most areas of South Africa.

Many orchids are also found in India, where numerous species occur at different altitudes in the Himalayas, mostly in the valleys and foothills. This proves that there is a large and varied number of plants suited to different growing conditions.

With modern exploration and tourism and the governments of China and other neighbouring countries becoming more open to foreign travellers, many new species, especially slipper orchids, have been discovered in south-western China in the last twenty years. Other countries where numerous new orchid species have been discovered include Vietnam, Laos and Cambodia.

Orchids grown in cultivation are generally epiphytes, which means that they grow on trees. However, orchids are not parasites and do not feed on the host trees - they simply use the trees as a support and do not generally harm the tree in any way. Orchids are also found as terrestrials, which means they grow in soil, or in the forest floor humus, but these are normally slightly more difficult to maintain in cultivation, luckily with several exceptions. Orchids are also sometimes found growing as lithophytes, which means they grow on rocks, and as (very rarely) saprophytes - where they feed on decaying organic matter. The genus *Rhizanthella*, found in Australia, even grows totally underground, with only the barest part of the flower itself ever emerging above ground. Certainly orchids have a varied and interesting range of habitats and growth habits to intrigue even the most intrepid gardener.

Orchids are not for the impatient gardener. Most species and hybrids take approximately 4-7 years from seed to flowering. In some instances they may even take up to 15 years or longer. Fortunately these plants are quite rare, and this is not the norm. Orchid seeds are extremely tiny and almost dust-like, and have no storage facility to assist in their germination. In nature, they only germinate in symbiotic association with a mycorrhizal fungus, which is also found in orchid roots. Because of this, a process has been developed whereby, in modern times, orchid seeds are germinated in laboratory conditions.

The orchid seeds are sown in flasks containing a sterile agar jelly, and are then grown in sterile conditions under artificial light till they are large enough to be transplanted into a normal potting medium. This process is fairly time-consuming and expensive, and is the reason why orchid seedlings can be expensive. Orchid plants are easy to propagate vegetatively by division. (See Chapter 6 for guidelines on how to divide your plants.) Many types of orchid also produce keikis or baby plantlets, and these can be removed from the mother plant when they are large enough and have sufficient roots to enable them to survive on their own.

Paphiopedilum rothschildianum - this species can take more than 15 years from seed to flowering

Cymbidium Oakbank

2
Basic Botanical Information on Orchids

Cymbidium Rocky Creek "Tregarthen" - showing typical orchid flower form

The Structure of the Flower

Orchids are different from other flowering plants in that they have a column as a central reproductive organ. In the column, the male and female reproductive organs have been fused in a single complex structure, making orchid flowers different from other flowers that have separate stamens and pistils. The pollination of orchid flowers is therefore specialized, and normally it would require a specific insect, be it a bee, ant or fly, endemic to the area where the plant occurs, to fertilise it. Some orchids also have very specialized mechanisms to ensure pollination by the correct pollinator.

Orchid flowers have a different floral configuration as well. The outer whorl of three segments which enclose the bud are called the sepals, and these three sepals normally look similar to one another. In the inner whorl of three petals, two petals are the same but again look different to the sepals. The third petal is specialized and looks different to the other petals, as well as the sepals. This specialized petal is called the "lip" in the majority of orchid species, and is usually bigger and more brightly coloured than the other petals. It serves to attract the pollinator to the column, which arises from the base of the floral segments.

In some species, the lip is smaller or almost insignificant, and the flower relies on another method of attracting the pollinator, either by scent (or smell) or the colour of the flower.

In some species, the sepals may be fused, further confusing the issue. In the slipper orchids, the lip is highly specialized to form a "slipper" shape, which forms part of the pollination mechanism of the flower.

Disa graminifolia - showing atypical flower form with hooded dorsal and insignificant petals

The different Types of Orchid Flowers and their Parts

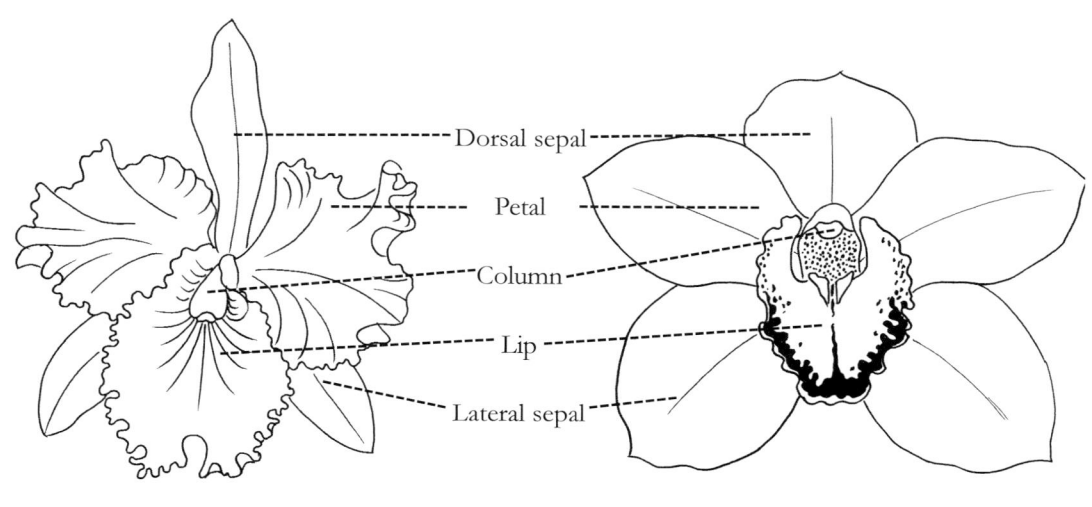

Cattleya *Cymbidium*

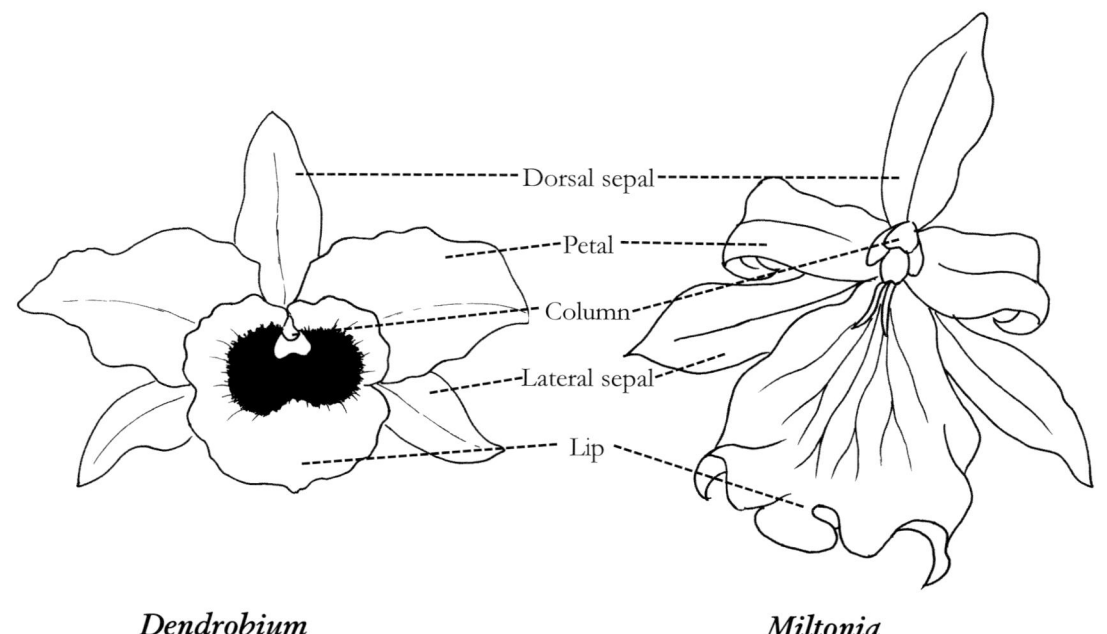

Dendrobium *Miltonia*

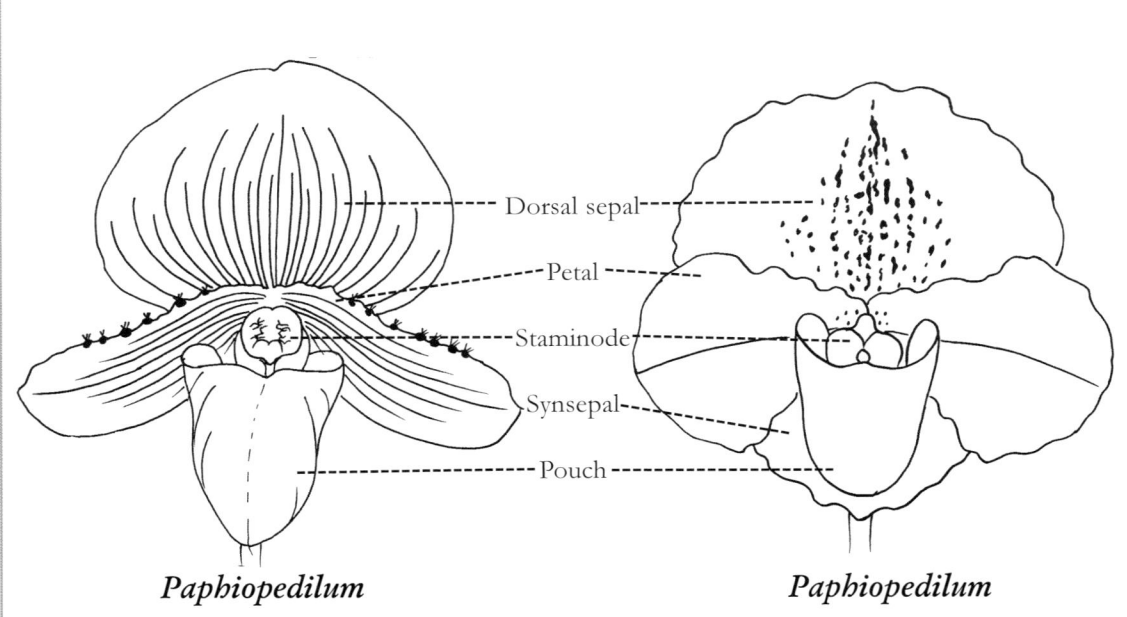
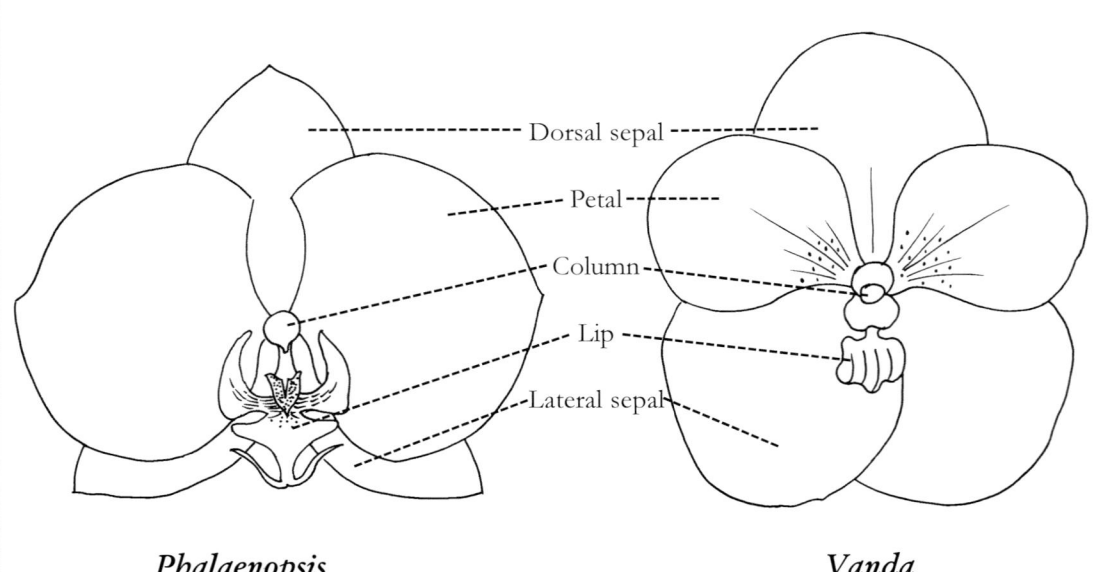

Growth Types

Orchids have a number of different types of growth habits. However, while they may appear different, they are basically variations of two types, namely sympodial and monopodial growth.

Monopodial Growth

In this instance, the orchid plant basically grows upright or vertically. The leaves appear around a central stem, and there is normally only one growth point. Flower stems appear from the base or side of the often woody stem. If the growing point of the plant is damaged, it may kill the plant. In some cases new plantlets may form at the base of the old stem, but this is not a given. As flower stems emerge from the side of the plant, this does not affect the growing point of the plant. Plants with monopodial growth have no water storage systems, and therefore often occur in areas with very high humidity and constant and reliable rainfall. Some examples of this group are the genera *Vanda, Arachnis, Phalaenopsis* and their related genera.

Sympodial Growth

Orchids with sympodial growth habits mostly grow horizontally from a creeping rhizome. These plants often have some type of fleshy cane or pseudobulb (bulb-like growth which is a storage mechanism) where the leaves mostly emerge from the top of the pseudobulb or cane, and in some cases form around the pseudobulb. These plants do have a water storage facility, and are usually found in areas where there are specific dry seasons or longer periods without rain. They often have multiple live eyes or leads that sprout new bulbs or canes from many of these eyes, forming large plants quickly. If a new growth is damaged in any way, a dormant eye will normally sprout with new growth.

Flower stems may emerge from the base of the cane or pseudobulb, or from the top or apex of the growth. Some examples of this group are *Cattleya, Cymbidium, Oncidium, Miltonia, Paphiopedilum* and their related genera. Certain genera, such as *Epidendrum*, especially the reed-stem types, and also the genus *Dendrobium*, may have monopodial growth habits in individual growths, but these form along a rhizome and one will have numerous growths from the base of the plant.

Monopodial Growth Habit

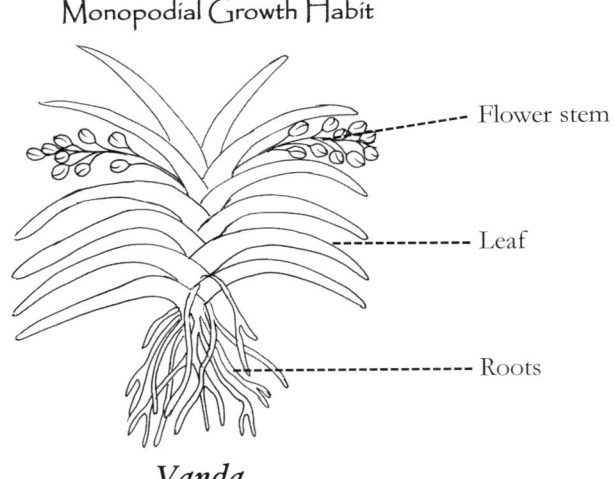

Vanda

Sympodial Growth Habit

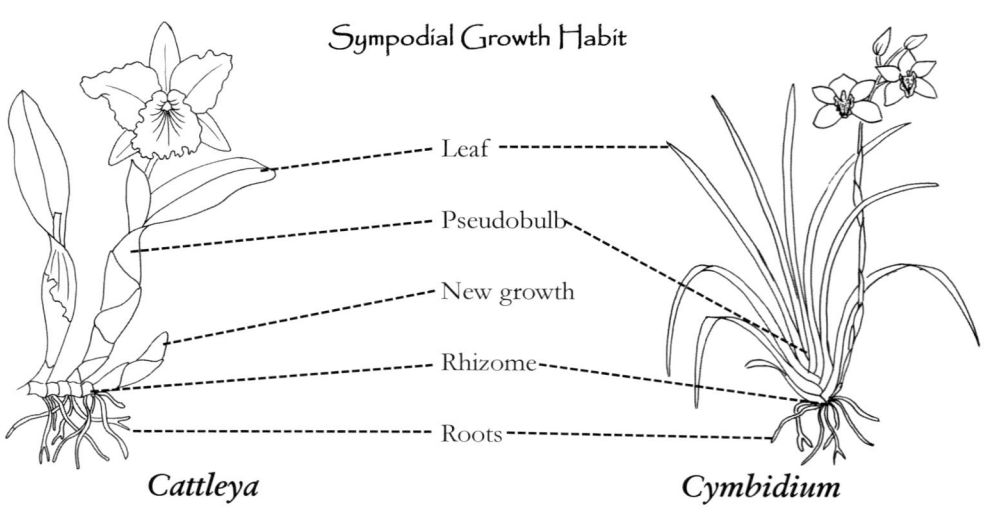

Cattleya — *Cymbidium*

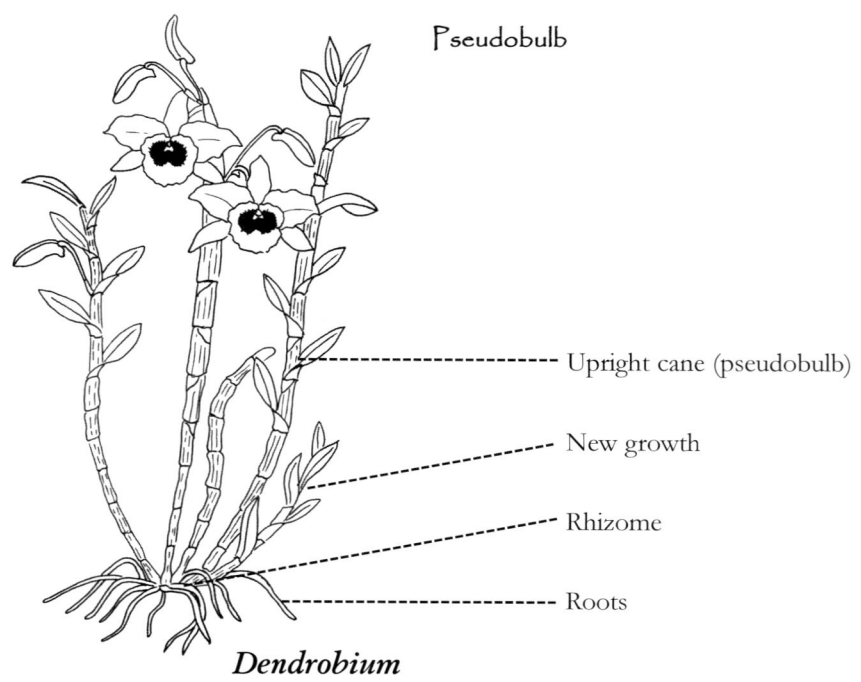

Dendrobium

Flowering Habits

Orchids generally flower only once a year, although well-grown plants of genera like *Vanda* may flower three to four times a year. Some *Cattleya* hybrids may flower twice a year. In general however, the lack of numerous flowerings is negated by the long-lasting nature of the flowers. Most orchid flowers will last 2-4 weeks on the plant, but many genera have flowers that last for up to four months on the plant.

Glossary of Terms

Some botanical and scientific terms will be used throughout this book. In order to facilitate the reader's understanding of these terms, a glossary is provided.

Aerial roots - referring to roots which are exposed to the air, and which may or may not be attached to the substrate on which the plant is growing

Apex - the tip of a floral segment furthest from the base, or the top of a plant

Apical - referring to the uppermost tip of a leaf or growth, appearing at or from the apex

Backbulb - an old cane or pseudobulb, which may or may not have leaves

Basal - referring to leaves or flower stems occurring from the base of a growth or pseudobulb

Cane - the growth of a plant which resembles a cane. Leaves may emerge along the sides or from the top. These canes may be thin, slightly thickened or even club-shaped, and grow upright

Column - central column-shaped structure which contains both the male and female reproductive organs, typical of the orchid family

Cultivar - this is the name given to a horticulturally selected specimen of a species or hybrid. This particular plant has some superior characteristics which are desirable, and the plant is thus identified. All future divisions (vegetative and by meristem propagation) bear this name, e.g. *Cattleya skinneri* "Lilac Dream", "Lilac Dream" being the cultivar name

Dormant/dormancy/dormant period - refers to the period in which a plant may be resting and not actively growing, normally the cold or otherwise dry season

Dorsal sepal - the uppermost sepal in an orchid flower opposite the lip

Epiphyte - a plant which grows on another plant without harming it

Flower spike - long, thin stem with no leaves, on which flowers are formed

Genus - a subdivision of a plant family, which contains all the species of that family which are related by certain characteristics. The plural is genera

Grex - a hybrid between two species or hybrids which has been given a specific name, and which is registered with the RHS

Habitat - the actual area where a certain orchid species is found. It refers to the aspect in which the plant is found, as well as the climatic conditions of the region to which the plant has adapted itself

Inflorescence - a term used to refer to the flower spike or flower stem

Intergeneric - a hybrid made up of more than one genus, and which can mean that from two up to six related genera occur in the background of an intergeneric hybrid

Keiki - a Hawaiian word which describes new plantlets forming at the base of a plant, along the flower stem, or which may appear in the place of flowering nodes, especially in certain *Dendrobium* species and hybrids

Lateral sepal - the two sepals in an orchid flower which are on either side of the lip

Lip/labellum - specialized petal in orchid flowers which often frames or highlights the column

Lithophyte - a plant growing on rocks, mostly exposed to the elements

Medium - a growing mix made up specifically for the growing of a certain type of plant

Mericlone - a name given to a plant which has been propagated vegetatively under laboratory conditions from the meristem (growing tip) of the mother plant, such plants being genetically identical to the mother plant. This is done in the case of rare or superior plants

Laeliocattleya Nora's Melody - showing peloria where the petals mimic the lip colour

Monopodial - growth habit of plants which is basically vertical, often with only one growing point which remains active for the life span of the plant

Mount - this refers to something upon which a plant is mounted in order to support it. In orchids, this is normally a branch or slab of bark, or even a live tree

Natural hybrid - a hybrid which has occurred naturally in the wild through insect pollination

Node - part of a cane or stem from which leaves or flowers may emerge

Peloria/peloric - an instance where the two petals of the orchid flower mimic the lip to look similar, often giving rise to splashes of contrasting colour on the petals, when the lip is not fully copied. This gives rise to the term "splash petals"

Pendent - hanging, referring to leaves or flower spikes which are not upright

Pseudobulb - referring to bulb-like structures which are observed in orchid plants. These "bulbs" are not true bulbs, but are the storage systems of the plant

Rhizome - a thickened fibrous structure that normally grows horizontally and which contains live eyes from where new growths emerge upward and new roots downward. In orchids, the rhizome is normally above the substrate upon which the plant is growing

Rupicolous - referring to plants which grow on or among rocks or in rocky soil, often in between other plants and grasses

Saprophyte - a plant which feeds on decaying organic matter

Splash petals - see *peloria/peloric*

Staminode - this organ is only seen in the slipper orchids, and forms the apex of the column. It shields the reproductive organs, which are located behind it

Substrate - the potting mixture in which the plant grows, or any other surface upon which the plant grows

Sympodial - the growth habit of plants where new growths form along a central rhizome, often with several growing points emerging in different directions

Synsepal - referring to the lateral sepals which are fused into one, as found in the slipper orchids

Terete - referring to leaves which are thin and equal, pencil-shaped along their length

Terrestrial - refers to plants which are found growing in soil, or in forest floor humus

Tribe - group of related orchid genera which share certain basic characteristics which set them apart from other tribes

Type species - the first species described in the genus, thus establishing the type of identification required for subsequently described species to be included in the genus

Velamen - a sponge-like covering, white in appearance, which surrounds orchid roots and which assists in water absorption and protection of exposed roots

Paphiopedilum insigne

3
General Growing Information

Traditionally, orchids have been known as difficult to grow, or as "hothouse" plants. This is not true, although there are, of course, species or genera which may need special growing conditions, or some which are not happy to be grown outside their natural habitat. This may be because they have very specific needs that occur only in their natural habitat, and which may be difficult or almost impossible to create artificially.

Oncidium sphacelatum growing in a handy tree fork

There are nevertheless literally thousands of orchid species and hybrids which are very well suited to being grown in a hothouse, shadehouse or simply outside in the garden. Provided the basic requirements are met, the gardener can be rewarded with lush growth and spectacular flowers year round from orchids selected for this purpose. All plant families have their own requirements for proper cultivation, and orchids are no exception.

In South Africa, we are very lucky to have a wide variety of climatic conditions which suit a number of different orchid genera. Sadly, not everything will grow everywhere, but again, isn't it true of all plant families? Often limited success will be good enough, but with orchids you have so much variety to choose from that the average gardener can have very good results.

The basic requirements are just what they say they are - the very basic needs of the plant in order to fulfill its needs to grow and flower. These include the growth medium, water, light, air movement, temperature, humidity and feeding/fertilizing.

A *Bulbophyllum* species growing lithophytically on a rock

Growth Medium

Orchids will grow in and on a variety of media. The most commonly grown species and hybrids in cultivation tend to be epiphytic, which means in nature they grow on trees - either on branches or on the trunk of the tree itself.

Lithophytic plants may be treated the same way in cultivation as epiphytic plants, as these two are often interchangeable in nature - it just depends on where the seed of the plant germinated. Plants which are able to grow lithophytically tend to be very hardy and will often tolerate extremely harsh conditions.

Epiphytic plants in cultivation can be grown on slabs of bark, normally pine bark or cork. They can also be mounted directly onto a living tree. These plants may also be grown in containers. Baskets (wooden slats, or even wire or plastic baskets) can be used with great success. The baskets must be filled with appropriately-sized bark chips to secure the plant inside. Plastic and clay pots can also be used, and epiphytes can be grown in these pots with bark chips sized to suit the plant.

Pine bark has to be used as it does not degrade too quickly, and it is relatively easy to obtain from nurseries and garden supply stores. *Pinus roxburghii* bark is preferable, but *Pinus patula* bark will do as well. However, it does not last as well as the former.

Bark mounts or slabs must be relevant to the size of the plant - do not mount a tiny seedling on a huge piece of bark, as the bark will start to degrade long before the plant reaches maturity and flowering size. Bark chips must also be relevant to the age of the plant, and in the case of mature plants the bark chip size must relate to the diameter of the roots. Seedlings should be planted in seedling grade bark chips, which should be 3-5 millimetres in size. Mature plants with fine roots (e.g. *Miltonia* and *Oncidium*) should be planted in bark chips of some 5-10 millimetres. Medium rooted plants such as *Cattleya* can be planted in medium size bark chips, which would be 10-15 millimetre chunks. Thick rooted plants such as *Cymbidium* and the *Vanda* tribe should be planted in large chunks of bark of some 15-25 millimetres in size. Most *Vanda* species and hybrids can in fact be grown in a basket without any bark medium inside at all, but one must then ensure adequate humidity and frequent watering.

Pine bark contains lots of tannins which may be detrimental to the quick rooting of the plant in the container. It is recommended that newly purchased bark be soaked in water for several days to leach out the tannins and artificially age the bark. Change the water at least twice in four days before using the bark, to ensure best results with the rooting of newly potted plants.

Various different types of epiphytic orchids growing on a tree - note the roots attaching themselves to the outside of the bark

Oncidium sphacelatum in a flowerbed in the Durban Botanical Gardens

Stanhopea wardii growing in a basket suspended from a tree

Watering

The cause of death of the majority of plants in cultivation is probably over-watering by ardent orchid growers. Orchids want to be cared for, but they do not want to be coddled and pampered too much. Regular thorough watering is important, rather than constantly giving the plants a little water every day. Again, this is similar to garden plants which would prefer thorough watering every few days. As we are growing these plants in places unlike their natural habitat, we have to ensure that they get the water they need to survive and grow.

If you grow your plants in containers, fill at least the bottom third of the pot with crocks to ensure proper drainage and stability for the pot. Orchid roots "breathe", and must be able to take up oxygen. Therefore, the mix in which they are planted must never be soggy or constantly wet. Proper drainage is also essential to ensure that the mix in the pots does not become stagnant or sour. This will kill the roots of the plants and lead to the death of the plant if not caught in time. Never let an orchid plant stand in a tray of water, as this will cause the breakdown of the potting medium and harm the plant. Harmful mineral salts also leach out of the mix and go to the surface of the potting mix if plants are allowed to stand in water. This forms a white "crust" on top of the potting mix, which will eventually kill the plant.

A good general rule is to water thoroughly at least twice a week in spring and summer, and once a week in autumn. Once in ten days is probably enough for winter, but this depends on the temperature in the area where you reside. If it is very cold with frost, once in ten days on sunny days should be enough. In warmer and even subtropical areas, watering in winter should be done at least once a week, more often if required. If it is hot and dry, water your plants. As long as plants have adequate drainage and pots can dry out between waterings, you will not overwater. Occasional misting of the leaves and roots during very hot and dry periods will be beneficial to your plants, especially epiphytes mounted on bark or growing in baskets. It is recommended that, in summer, you mist at least once a day on days when you are not watering, as this will cool down the plants, and will also help to increase the ambient humidity.

Be careful not to water deciduous plants in winter, at least not until they have started sprouting in spring. Dormant plants or those undergoing a winter resting period can be misted or even watered occasionally in winter, as this will prevent the plant from becoming too dehydrated. Remember that orchid plants do not generally wilt, as the leaves are too hardy. If you experience wilting in orchid plants you should immediately check the root system - if the roots have died the plant will wilt much faster than when it is suffering from a lack of water. In the case of dead roots, repot immediately in fresh potting mix and keep the plant cool and in a shady place for 3-4 weeks. Mist regularly, as this may encourage fresh root growth.

Plants should preferably be watered early in the day to ensure that they have dried off by nightfall. Wet plants can easily be infected by bacteria and fungal spores, as the cooler temperatures at night can reduce the plants' ability to fight infection.

Disa uniflora in its habitat on Table Mountain

Note: Refer also to the chapter on repotting for advice on how to select the proper size pot to suit the type and size of plant.

Arundina graminifolia as a garden plant

General Growing Information

Paphiopedilum insigne on a rotting log in a shady spot

Humidity

Humidity is very important to the successful cultivation of orchids outside their natural habitat. The sponge-like velamen of aerial orchid roots can absorb moisture from the air when the plant requires it, provided the humidity is high enough. High humidity also prevents water loss from the leaf cells and keeps the plants sturdy. Low humidity may dry out plants too quickly and cause them to become wilted and desiccated.

Improve the humidity around your orchids by doing the following:

- Grow companion plants such as bromeliads and ferns around your orchids
- Grow *Selaginella* on the ground in shady areas, or under shade house benching
- Water the ground below your orchids, as the evaporation increases humidity without the orchids becoming wet too
- On very hot days, mist the air around your plants with water from a pressure sprayer or by using the mister setting on your hosepipe
- Grow your mounted epiphytes suspended over or near a fish pond

A novel way of growing an orchid on a tree

Eulophia angolensis grows in swampy conditions

Light

The importance of the correct amount of light for the successful growing and flowering of orchids cannot be over-emphasised. Insufficient light is the main reason why orchid plants do not flower. The majority of orchids will not do well indoors, as they do require some exposure to sunlight. Sunlight matures the new growths of the plants to levels where they are strong enough to flower, and also encourages the growth of the actual flower spike. Orchids grow in cycles and generally flower only once a year, so it is worth your while to ensure that your plants get the opportunity to do so!

The light requirements of orchids range from almost full shade to various degrees of dappled sunlight or shading, and in some instances even full sunlight. As a general rule, orchids should not be exposed to the harshest period of sunshine around midday, although many of the hardier species and hybrids will tolerate it, provided the humidity is high enough. Most orchids are not as easy to kill as many people seem to think - a constant battery of poor care over weeks is needed to kill an orchid, but if you put a shade-loving orchid out into the full sun on a summer day, you will damage it.

Orchid species and hybrids of different genera do have different light requirements. As a general rule, conditions of about 30-40% shade throughout the day will suit the vast majority of plants commercially grown and available to the general public in South Africa. Kindly refer to the chapter: Orchids by Genus for more detailed information on the shade and light requirements and tolerances of the plants you are interested in growing.

Air movement

Air movement is important for all plants, not only orchids. Plants are living organisms which require a good exchange of air in order to ensure their health. During the day, plants of all types combine light and oxygen to form sugars and other required substances for their survival, and this process gives off carbon dioxide. At night, the process of respiration is reversed. Carbon dioxide is absorbed by plants and oxygen given off.

It is important for growers to provide ample air movement around plants, to ensure constant delivery of the required gases to the plants, and the removal of whatever gas is given off by the plant at that time. A gentle breeze is sufficient, and is most often present in the garden. Plants grown indoors should be placed close to a window, not only for the available light, but also for access to proper ventilation. Orchid plants in particular do not do well in buildings with air-conditioning, as this process removes moisture from the air and dehydrates plants. A constant supply of fresh, moving air also dries off excess moisture from plant leaves, and ensures that fungal spores and bacteria do not linger and get the opportunity to infect the plants. A fresh and buoyant atmosphere is best.

Angraecum superbum and *Angraecum eburneum* growing in full sun in flowerbeds

◀ Opposite page: *Phaius tankervilleae* with arum lilies in a flowerbed

Phalaenopsis hybrid growing in a tree in Durban – only attempt this in warm and sheltered areas

Temperature

The biggest fallacy about orchids is that they are all hothouse plants. Whilst there are some plants that do require such conditions, they are the minority. Most orchids grow and flourish when grown at temperatures from 12-32°C. This is considered to be the intermediate range of temperatures. Cool growing plants thrive in the range of temperatures from 5-18°C, and warm growing plants should be grown in the range 18-32°C. Apart from a very few exceptions, the majority of plants discussed in this book will fall in the intermediate range, sometimes with indications that a plant should be in the higher, or lower part of that range. Most plants discussed will do well in the entire range.

In fact, 32°C is considered to be the uppermost limit of temperatures that orchid plants should be exposed to, as efficient respiration and food production by the plants are adversely affected at temperatures higher than this. Luckily, plants are adaptable and resilient, and will cope if subjected to higher temperatures for short periods. Where plants have been

exposed to higher temperatures, the often cooler night temperatures will help them to recover, and high humidity and good air movement will also assist in the recovery.

Shading plants during very hot and sunny weather will assist in bringing down the temperature they are exposed to. Orchid leaves should never feel hot to the touch. If they do, they are exposed to too much sun and must be sheltered. Most orchid plants' leaves are perennial, and sunburn damage will show on the plant for many years. Misting the plants with water during very high temperatures will also be beneficial to increase humidity and cool the plants, and the evaporation of water around the plants will also decrease the temperature around them, even if only for a short time.

Very few plants like to be subjected to temperatures below freezing, and orchids are no exception. Even the hardiest orchids are not immune to severe frost, but may survive light frost. Most plants in the intermediate and cool-growing range will withstand exposure to low temperatures for short periods of time with no significant harmful side effects. This is of course provided the plants were not too wet at the time the frost occurred - another reason for ensuring plants are watered early in the day. If a cold front is expected, rather do not water at all - dry plants are far less likely to suffer ill effects from a cold spell. Black frost spells disaster for all plants that are exposed to it, so be sure to take care to shelter sensitive plants if such an event is foreseen.

Cattleya aurantiaca as a rockery plant in a subtropical garden

Ensure that your orchids are not at risk of exposure to frost and cold winds by growing them in a sheltered spot, or, if possible, by moving them to a sheltered place like a covered patio during very cold weather.

Feeding your Orchids

Opinions vary about what to feed orchids during the various times in their growing season. Fact is, all orchids will benefit from regular feeding to ensure they have the proper minerals and other nutrients they need to grow and flower properly. Any good nursery or garden centre will be able to advise growers on the available chemical and organic fertilisers that are suitable for use on orchid plants. Try to get a balanced general fertiliser, and use according to the manufacturer's instructions. In general, feeding fortnightly with a liquid fertiliser is recommended. This can be applied with a watering can or with a pressure sprayer, which can also be obtained from garden centres or nurseries. Feeding is best done in the morning, which will allow the plants the entire day to assimilate the nutrients in the fertiliser.

Growers can use chemical fertilisers which are made up of various components to promote either good growth or a spectacular flush of flowers. General fertilisers can be used throughout the year. Organic fertilisers can be used with good effect, and include those made up of seaweed extract or fish emulsions. It is not advisable to use guano or other forms of manure, as these may be too strong and can harm the plants and their root systems.

Feeding should be done once in two weeks, and if liquid based, should replace a regular watering. Slow-release granules (normally a general fertiliser) can be used, again according to the manufacturer's instructions. These should be applied at the start of the growing season in spring. Supplementing it with a liquid fertiliser will be beneficial, as the granules do seem to degrade faster than suggested.

Laelia anceps grown mounted on a tree

It is advisable to contact an expert grower in your area who is a member of an orchid society, and to hear from him or her what works best for them. Orchid growers are normally friendly people who are always happy to talk about their plants and how to grow them. Contact information for South African Orchid Council affiliated societies appear at the back of this book. Some recommended fertilisers are Chemicult, Multifeed, Seagro, Kelpak, Nitrosol and Trelmix. Limited applications of compost and BounceBack can also be used for terrestrial orchids.

Pests and Diseases

Orchids are susceptible to a number of pests and diseases, but luckily most of them are easily treated. Thrips, aphids and greenfly are commonly seen, as are soft brown scale and mealy bug. All of these can be treated with the application of an orchid-approved systemic insecticide such as Chlorpyrifos or Malathion. This would normally solve the problem after 2-3 applications, but do be extremely careful when working with systemic poisons. They can enter your body by means of your skin, and are very harmful to your health.

Rather use the following: Mix one litre of lukewarm water, one teaspoon of liquid detergent, and one tablespoon of methylated spirits. Spray the affected plants and areas with this solution. It is not harmful to the plant, and will be washed off at the next watering. It is, however, not a permanent or long-term solution to the problem, and will have to be re-applied as needed.

Upon treatment, thrips, greenfly and aphids will go away, as will mealy bug, but dead soft brown scale must be removed with an old toothbrush. When dealing with mealy bugs, make sure that you spray all crevices and folds in leaves as these pernicious bugs hide very well and are difficult to eradicate. They are especially prevalent in all indoor plants.

Red spider mites and false mites tend to attack the softer leaved types such as *Miltonia* and *Oncidium*. They often occur where there is a lack of humidity in the growing area. It is best to use a systemic insecticide to kill these pests,

Vanda Miss Joaquim in full sun in the Durban Botanical Gardens

Miltonia spectabilis "Abigail"

and ensure that humidity in the area is increased to avoid having the problem again.

Slugs and snails and other common garden pests can be treated in any manner which you have found successful in the past. If your problems with pests persist, contact an expert orchid grower or your garden centre or nursery for advice.

Orchids are not often attacked by diseases, but sometimes bacterial soft rot or fungal infections may occur. These should be treated after obtaining advice from an expert, as the various infections are not all that easy to tell apart. Treatment with chemicals such as Physan or Dursban may be recommended. Often one only needs to cut away the infected part and treat the cut edges with flowers of sulphur. This may stop the rot from growing and infecting the rest of the plant. If a plant is badly affected, discard it before the problem spreads to other plants in the area.

Orchids are sometimes affected by a number of viruses. These are indicated by unusual but recognizable markings on the leaves, or can be indicated by "colour break", where unexpected blotches and markings of colour appear on the flowers. Viruses easily spread when contaminated cutting instruments spread the sap from infected plants to healthy ones. Always disinfect or sterilise cutting instruments after each plant they are used on. Viruses cannot be treated and never go away - infected plants should be discarded and preferably burnt to destroy them. Contact an expert orchid grower or the Botany Department of your local university if you are in any doubt about viruses in your orchids. Your local nursery or garden centre will most likely not be able to help you. Remember - there is no cure - infected plants must be destroyed.

Phalaenopsis amabilis

4

Orchids by Genus – General Cultural Information

As the various orchid genera share basically the same cultural requirements, a number of the more commonly grown ones will be discussed. Some general information pertaining to each will be highlighted. As certain species and hybrids may have slightly different requirements, individual plants are discussed in Chapter 5. If a grower knows only the genus of the plant in his possession, following these general guidelines should be useful in growing and flowering such a plant

The Cattleya Alliance

The genus *Cattleya* is commonly found in cultivation, often in the trade. Most of these plants occur from sea-level up to the lower montane forests in South and Central America, and can generally be grown under intermediate growing conditions. Most species occur below 1 000 metres, with only a few up to 1 500 metres and sometimes higher.

Cattleya species and hybrids are sturdy, vigorous plants. They flower throughout the year, but mostly in spring and autumn. They require high light levels at all times, with a recommended average shading of 30 percent. Average to high humidity and good air movement will benefit the plants, which will normally not flower if they are grown in too much shade. Growths should be firm and upright and should have a solid green colour. Lanky or soft growths may indicate too much shade.

These plants grow actively in spring and summer and must be watered and fed regularly to promote good growth. Winter is generally their dormant or resting season when the growths mature. During this time, water sparingly and do not feed the plants. Resume active watering and feeding once new growth appears in spring.

Shield plants from frost or cold winds in winter. The recommended potting mix is pine bark chunks appropriate to the size of the plants. There are several genera of orchids in the *Cattleya* family which share similar cultivation requirements. These include the genera *Epidendrum, Encyclia, Laelia, Brassavola* and *Schomburgkia*.

Laeliocattleya Irene Holguin

Cymbidium Seagem "Wildroot"

Cymbidium

The genus *Cymbidium* is commonly grown by gardeners and orchid growers and is often sold as cut flowers or pot plants, as the flowers last exceptionally long. These species originate in the East from countries such as India, Thailand and China, and are generally tolerant of intermediate conditions. *Cymbidium* hybrids like high light intensities and can be grown in full sun for most of the day, although it is recommended that some shading is available during midday to avoid sunburn damage to the leathery leaves. Plants will not initiate flower stems if nights are too warm in autumn, and the grower can attempt to lower the temperature at night by watering around, but NOT on the plants in the early evening. A difference between day and night temperatures of 15°C in autumn is recommended for proper flower initiation.

Cymbidiums are heavy feeders and require ample watering and feeding throughout spring and summer to ensure maximum growth. Watering in autumn and winter should be limited to once a week, with no feeding until new growth starts in spring. These plants tolerate cold well, but not frost. Severe cold may damage flower buds, so be sure to shield plants in spike from cold winds. The plants need lots of light in winter, to ensure that the long flower spikes are strong enough to carry the weight of the large flowers.

Flowering depends on the type of species or hybrid, but miniature and early-flowering *Cymbidium* plants may flower from late summer to early autumn, and standard plants from early spring to early summer. The recommended potting mix is equal parts of medium to large pine bark chunks, commercial potting soil and washed river sand. Some nurseries may stock *Cymbidium* mix.

Dendrobium

The genus *Dendrobium* is one of the largest orchid genera and has many different sections, all of which may require totally different cultivation conditions. The species of this genus occur from India, Thailand and surrounding countries, down to Papua New Guinea and Australia. They are often referred to as Australasian species. Only three of these sections and their hybrids are generally available in the trade, and these will be discussed below. If you are not sure which type of *Dendrobium* you have, contact an orchid society in your area for advice, or ask a grower at a local orchid show.

Dendrobium nobile types (soft cane)

These species are from India and surrounding areas, and have so-called soft canes. They grow well in intermediate conditions, and can withstand some cooler temperatures. Numerous colourful hybrids have been made in this section, and all are easy to grow in the garden. These plants grow vigorously in their growing season during spring and summer, and as the plants originate from the monsoon areas which get almost no rain in the dry winter months, they are especially suitable as garden plants in the summer rainfall areas of South Africa.

Dendrobium nobile

Dendrobium nobile and its hybrids like average to good humidity and sufficient air movement. They are gross feeders and will do well with regular applications of liquid fertiliser. Plants normally grow as epiphytes on trees and should be mounted in such a way as to receive the maximum amount of sunlight to ensure good growth. They can also be mounted on deciduous trees where they will receive the proper amount of light they require in winter to harden and mature the new pseudobulbs. They only need to be shaded from the hottest sun on summer days to avoid burning the leaves, and are tolerant of cold in winter. As with most orchids, they should not be exposed to frost. The soft and pliable leaves of these types are a light to dark glossy green, while the stems are firm, but not woody and hard.

These *Dendrobium* species and hybrids need only the lightest watering or misting during the dry winter months, and growers should not feel sorry for the plants and water them during this time. An excess of water in the dry season will prevent flowers from forming on the pseudobulb nodes, and instead of flowers, plantlets or keikis will appear along the pseudobulb. Give only enough water to prevent the plant from desiccating, and do not be concerned if the pseudobulbs shrivel slightly during this time - it is quite normal. In late winter to spring, the flower buds will appear along the leaf nodes on the pseudobulbs. Resume normal watering and feeding once you are able to see the actual flower buds forming, and not before this time.

Growers in the winter rainfall season of South Africa should preferably grow these plants under cover in winter, but must ensure that sufficient sunlight reaches the plants. A translucent roof of Perspex, fibreglass or plastic sheeting can be used, but once the buds have formed, the plants can be exposed to the elements again.

In the winter rainfall area, it may be advisable to grow this type of plant in pots so that they may be moved easily.

Although Dendrobiums are best grown mounted on trees, they do as well in slatted baskets, or in plastic or clay pots. In a pot or basket, they should be grown in medium-sized chunks of pine bark. Very good drainage must be provided to allow roots to dry out between waterings. *Dendrobium* plants do best when underpotted, in other words, plant them in the smallest pot that you can fit the roots into. An excess of available mix in the pots stays wet for too long after watering, and this may cause the roots and new growths to rot.

Dendrobium Pravith White

Dendrobium bigibbum type (hard cane)

These species and hybrids are warmer growing and prefer high humidity and warm temperatures all year round. They like lots of sunlight, and in tropical and subtropical areas can be grown outdoors. They can be grown mounted on trees, but it is recommended that growers in the colder areas of South Africa grow this type of *Dendrobium* in pots. This would enable the grower to move the plants to a more sheltered position at the onset of winter, as they are highly susceptible to cold and frost. They can be watered and fed throughout the year, with only a slight reduction in the frequency in the cooler seasons to give the plants a resting period.

The *Dendrobium bigibbum* type of plants may require some extra care from the grower, but the reward is long sprays of large, colourful and very long-lasting flowers which emerge from close to the top of the pseudobulbs. The pseudobulbs and leaves are literally much harder than the nobile types. The leaves should be dark green and in fact almost purple as a result of exposure to ample light.

Dendrobium June Mac

When growing these plants in a pot, use medium-size pine bark chunks, and again be sure to underpot, placing the plant in the smallest pot it will fit into. As these plants can be very tall, place ample heavy crocks in the base of the pot to stabilise it, or anchor the pots in such a way that they will not blow over in the breeze. *Dendrobium bigibbum* and its hybrids generally flower in autumn and winter through to spring. Due to recent species name changes, this section was formerly known as the *Dendrobium phalaenopsis* section, as the flowers look similar to those of the genus *Phalaenopsis*.

The Australian Dendrobiums

There are several *Dendrobium* species which originate from Australia, and numerous hybrids have been made with them. These hybrids include *Dendrobium kingianum*, which is easy to grow and flower in cultivation. Although these plants require a slightly cooler winter in order to flower properly, they and their hybrids are easy to obtain and grow. In nature, this species and most of the others used in hybridising grow as epiphytes and lithophytes. They also grow well in gardens, mounted on trees, in pots or baskets, and even as rockery plants. They require ample water and feeding in spring and summer, with a cooler and drier resting period in winter. Too much water in winter may induce the formation of keikis rather than flowers, so do take care not to overwater.

The Australian Dendrobiums and hybrids prefer bright to full sunlight all year round. However, it is advisable to provide shelter against the harsh midday sun to prevent the leaves from burning. Good humidity and ample air movement are also beneficial. It cannot be stressed enough that orchids thrive in a buoyant and fresh environment. When potted, they should be grown in fine to medium pine bark chips as they do not have very thick roots. Provide enough drainage in pots to allow the roots the chance to dry out slightly between waterings, and not to stay wet for too long. They flower mostly in spring, and are hardy plants, tolerating cold spells. They should be protected from frost.

Paphiopedilum Leeanum - a green-leafed hybrid

Paphiopedilum

The slipper orchids generally require less light than most other orchid species. They thrive in shady conditions with at most dappled sunlight. *Paphiopedilums* are semi-terrestrial plants, and do not do well when mounted on bark or grown on trees.

They originate from the humid forests of the East, including countries such as India, Burma and Thailand. Here plants often grow in the forest litter, and rarely as epiphytes on trees. Some species grow on the limestone cliffs in Thailand, and have more specific cultural requirements. Several species also come from southern China, where they grow on cliff faces exposed to the elements.

The slipper orchids should preferably be potted, and must be grown in a well-drained mix of seedling to fine grade pine bark, mixed with about a third marble chips to provide stability. *Paphiopedilum* species and hybrids do not have extensive root systems, and also no water storage facility. They should be kept evenly moist all year round, and be fed regularly with half-strength liquid fertiliser.

Paphiopedilums will not tolerate cold and must be sheltered in winter if not grown in tropical and sub-tropical areas. They do very well as houseplants, but should never stand in water as this will cause the roots to rot.

Plants can broadly be divided into two categories with different temperature requirements. Those with plain, light-green leaves are intermediate growing and can tolerate cooler temperatures down to 5°C. Those with leaves that are darker green and where the leaves are overlaid with mauve/purple marbling or tessellations, have warmer temperature requirements. They should be sheltered in winter and should not be grown at temperatures below 12°C.

If you intend to grow your slipper orchids indoors, choose a room with some northern exposure to provide enough light. Grow the plants on top of trays filled with pebbles to catch excess water. The water evaporating from these trays will increase the humidity around the plants. The slipper orchids are one of the orchid families that absorb nutrients efficiently through their leaves. Ensure to rinse off the leaves regularly to keep them dust-free when grown indoors. Water and fertiliser sprayed on the leaves will be beneficial, but ensure a good enough air flow to allow the plants to dry off before evening. Repot the plants at least once a year, as fresh potting medium stimulates root growth.

Some species such as *Paphiopedilum insigne* and its allies, as well as other species and primary hybrids in the genus *Phragmipedium* can be grown outside in the garden in temperate and humid climates. Provide a shady spot that is regularly watered, and ensure that the soil is rich and friable, with pine bark mixed in to improve drainage. Slipper orchids flower throughout the year, but mostly in autumn and winter.

Phalaenopsis

The so-called moth orchids are very popular as house- and pot plants and are sold by numerous chain stores and nurseries when in flower. *Phalaenopsis* plants are often used in interior decorating because of the beautiful colours and long-lasting nature of the flowers. Plants can in fact be in flower for up to three months. These plants come from warm and

Paphiopedilum Maudiae - a mottled-leaf hybrid

humid areas in the East such as Thailand and the Philippines, where they grow as epiphytes in the rain forests.

These species and hybrids are epiphytes and must be grown in pots, with medium grade pine bark chunks. The pots should never be allowed to stand in water, as the plant roots do not like being soggy and wet. *Phalaenopsis* plants have very low light requirements and should be grown indoors or in a sheltered environment such as a greenhouse. They do not have any storage facilities, and must therefore be watered and fed throughout the year.

The plants prefer a very humid environment, so you may wish to keep your plants in the bathroom when not in flower. Growing them over a tray of pebbles filled with water will help to increase the humidity. Be sure to keep the leaves free from dust, and inspect your plants regularly for mealy bug. *Phalaenopsis* plants are very prone to attacks from this pest, which likes to feed on the succulent leaves and flower stems. Look for them in leaf axils and at flower nodes on the spikes, and treat the problem immediately, as the bugs spread rapidly to other plants in the area.

Phalaenopsis plants will quickly show the grower when they are not happy. The leaves should always be a dark, rich green, and should be firm and turgid to the touch. If the leaves are wilting or turning yellow, this may indicate a problem with the watering, or even indicate a loss of roots due to overwatering. Take immediate steps to rectify the problem or you may lose your plant. Bear in mind that the basal leaves only last for 2-3 years and that they do eventually die. This is natural and should not be a cause for concern, provided the plant still has several strong and healthy leaves.

The moth orchids do not appreciate cold at all and should be grown in as warm a place as possible. Do not keep them in a room with an air conditioner, as the latter dries out the air and creates cold draughts, both of which are harmful to the health of these plants. Although they thrive on a certain measure of care, *Phalaenopsis* plants are basically easy to grow and provide the grower with long-lasting flowers as a reward.

Phalaenopsis Brother Pico Chip

The Genus Vanda and its Allies

The genus *Vanda* and its related genera do quite well in tropical and subtropical gardens around South Africa, as they originate from the tropical East. In other temperate areas they can also be grown outside without shelter, provided they are not exposed to frost and cold winds. Vandas and their allies are generally gross feeders and can be watered and fed prolifically throughout the year, and as they do not have storage facilities other than their leaves, they prefer high humidity levels all year round. Plants in this alliance may flower throughout the year, and in fact most well-grown plants may flower 3-4 times, providing numerous colourful and long-lasting flowers. Mature plants can become quite tall. In colder areas, these plants will do best under cover in winter. Hybrids containing the species *Vanda coerulea* (generally lilac to pink/purple in colour) are more tolerant to cold.

The so-called strap-leaved types have the largest flowers, and long, narrow and flat leaves, similar in appearance to a leather strap. Hybrids are generally available in the trade. Vandas like bright light and can be grown in full sun, provided some shade is available during the hottest part of the day. Being less tolerant of cold, plants should be protected in winter. Certain genera such as *Arachnis* and *Renanthera* have similar requirements.

The terete-leaved species are more tolerant of cold, and can also be grown with ease in full sunlight. The leaves of these plants are short, thin, round and pencil-like in appearance. Hybrids between the two types are called semi-terete, and have shorter, v-shaped leaves. They can also be placed in full sunlight, but are less tolerant of cold.

There are numerous intergeneric hybrids (between related genera in this group), but these are mostly smaller plants, with some even being miniatures. These hybrids do best in light shade (30-40%) and like humid intermediate to warm conditions with some protection from cold in the winter.

This genus, its related genera and hybrids are extremely rewarding and easy to grow and flower, provided the basic cultural requirements are met.

All of these plants should be grown in pots or baskets with medium to large chunks of bark, suitable to the size of the plant and the thickness of the roots. Many hybrids have prolific aerial roots which will grow outside the container. These should not be forced into the container, but be left to grow at will, and must be watered and fed as well to ensure vigorous growth of the plant.

Vanda Carmen Coll - a strap-leafed hybrid

◀ Opposite Page: Vanda Miss Joaquim showing its terete leaves

Vanda Nellie Morley - a semi-terete hybrid

The *Miltonia/Oncidium* alliance

These two genera are closely related, with the pseudobulbs, leaves and flowers being very similar in appearance. There are numerous other genera related to these two, and they interbreed easily to form a number of intergeneric hybrids. These genera originate from South and Central America, and are found from the coastal forests at sea level, to the rain forests, and into the high elevation montane cloud forests. This means that the species and hybrids in these genera have a range of different cultural requirements, from warm and humid, to intermediate, and some are even quite cold-growing. The grower should therefore select the species and hybrids that he wishes to grow with care, as everything may not be suited to the conditions he can provide. The majority of the intergeneric hybrids can be grown under intermediate conditions, depending of course on the species in the background of these hybrids.

Miltonia x bluntii - a natural hybrid

In general, these species and hybrids have bulb-like pseudobulbs with one to two or more soft leaves at the top of the pseudobulbs. Flower stems normally emerge from between the basal leaves of the pseudobulbs, and different species and hybrids flower at different times throughout the year. Many hybrids and species have pleasant fragrances. The roots of these plants are normally quite fine and almost thread-like, indicating that they prefer a fine to medium grade potting medium, preferably 5-15 millimetre pine bark chunks. Many of the species and hybrids form rather large specimen plants over time, and these large plants may be planted in slightly larger pine bark chunks. Because of the fine nature of the roots, they should not be disturbed too often, so choose your pots in such a way that plants only need to be repotted every two to three years. The roots damage easily and care must be taken when handling the plants.

Most of the species and hybrids are well suited to being mounted on the side of trees where they will receive ample light. Good air movement and humidity are also essential, as the roots of mounted plants can dry out very quickly. Exposed roots on mounted plants often remain dry for long periods of time, and high humidity will alleviate this problem.

Take care to shelter the plants from too much direct sunlight as their somewhat softer leaves can burn easily. Feeding and watering can be applied copiously throughout the growing season of summer and spring, with a reduction of both in autumn and winter. Although feeding is not critical in the cooler months, water should be given once a week to avoid the pseudobulbs from shrivelling. Because of the soft leaves, red spider mite tends to attack these plants if the humidity is too low. Ensure that the humidity remains high, and treat the pest as indicated if it does occur. In general, these plants can tolerate some cold, but should be sheltered from frost and cold winds.

The species and hybrids in this alliance tend to be quite susceptible to the various viruses which may infect orchid plants. If you are unsure, get an expert opinion to find out if you have a problem. Should there be a virus on one of your plants, destroy it immediately, and always be sure to sterilise your cutting tools after working with each plant. Viruses are spread by the sap of affected plants.

Oncidium sphacelatum flowering spectacularly on a tree

Many species and hybrids in this group flower in spring and autumn, but with so many genera often involved with the hybrids, flowering may be at any time of the year when the new growths have matured. It is possible to get an impressive range of colours with the different hybrids and species available.

Phalaenopsis Flor de Niebla

5

Recommended Orchids

This chapter will introduce the reader to a range of orchid species and hybrids suitable for cultivation in gardens and shade houses. Some plants which may require more warmth and shelter will also be included, as these can be grown indoors.

Aerangis stylosa

Aerangis stylosa from Madagascar and the Comores is an intermediate to warm-growing plant. It requires shady, humid conditions (50-60% shade) and does best when mounted on a slab of bark, or onto the side of a tree trunk. Water and feed regularly throughout the year.

Shelter from frost and low temperatures and do not allow the plant to be exposed to temperatures below 8°C, as this will harm it. The crystalline white, scented flowers appear in spring and summer.

Angraecum leonis

Angraecum leonis is a compact-growing epiphyte which grows well under intermediate to warm conditions. It has almost succulent leaves and can withstand almost full sun throughout the day, although shading of 20-30% is recommended. This species prefers high humidity and good air movement, and can be watered and fed throughout the year. It does need some protection from cold, and should best be grown in a pot in fine to medium pine bark chunks in colder areas, so that it can be moved under shelter during cold weather. In tropical and subtropical areas, *Angraecum leonis* may be grown outdoors in a container, or even mounted on a tree or a piece of bark. The clear white, fragrant flowers appear in spring.

Angraecum sesquipedale

Angraecum sesquipedale is a rather robust and large-growing plant from Madagascar. It requires intermediate to warm conditions, and should be protected from low temperatures.

As plants form clumps and can exceed one metre in height, they should be grown in a shady spot at the base of a tree in a subtropical garden, or they can be grown in pots in similar shady and sheltered areas. Use medium to large pine bark chunks to provide a free-draining epiphytic mix. Water and feed regularly throughout the year, and provide humid conditions and good air movement. This species flowers in winter and spring and has large, 12-15 centimetre flowers which are highly scented.

Arachnis Maggie-Oei

This hybrid, as well as the species *Arachnis flos-aeris*, consists of intermediate to warm growing plants. The vine-like plants grow quite tall and need some form of staking or other support to keep them upright. Plants have short, leathery leaves tolerating full sunlight throughout the day, provided humidity is high and air movement brisk. Mist plants regularly in summer, and a daily drink will help to increase humidity. Feed regularly throughout the year. Although plants will tolerate low temperatures for short periods, shelter them from frost and cold winds. Plants can flower at any time all through the year.

Arundina graminifolia

Arundina graminifolia is a vigorous and tall-growing terrestrial species which can be grown as a garden plant in the frost-free areas of South Africa. It does best in sandy soil rich in compost, and can be cultivated in a container in a similar medium. It can be grown in full sun, but must be watered regularly throughout the year. Additional feeding can be given if the soil is not rich enough. It can grow to more than a metre tall and forms large clumps, which can be divided regularly. This species flowers throughout the year as the growths mature, and numerous large bright-pink flowers open successively on the flower spike which is at the apex of the reed-like growth.

Ascocentrum species

These charming miniature plants will grow and flower well in intermediate conditions, although they will do better in warmer areas. Keep them at temperatures above 8°C, and provide 30-40% shade. Although they are epiphytic and can be grown mounted on trees, they do best in small slatted baskets with medium-size pine bark chunks. Water and feed regularly throughout the year, and provide high humidity and good air movement. Flowering can occur at any time during the year, but mostly in spring and summer. These species have been extensively bred with the larger *Vanda* species to produce the medium sized *Ascocenda* hybrids which are easy-growing. See the *Vanda* section in this chapter for photographs of these and other hybrids. Recommended species are *Ascocentrum ampullaceum*, *Ascocentrum ampullaceum* var. *album*, *Ascocentrum curvifolium* and *Ascocentrum miniatum*.

Ascocentrum ampullaceum

Ascocentrum ampullaceum var. *album*

Ascocentrum curvifolium

Ascocentrum miniatum

Bifrenaria harrisoniae var. *alba*

Bifrenaria harrisoniae

Bifrenaria harrisoniae is a hardy South American plant with hard pseudobulbs and leathery leaves which tolerate full sun, with some shading being beneficial when it is very hot. It is an intermediate grower, but will tolerate low temperatures and mild frost. Water and feed regularly in the growing season, but keep the plant dry in winter as it undergoes a dormant period. Light watering once every 10-14 days in winter is ample to keep the plant healthy. Flowering is in spring from the base of the pseudobulbs, and the highly scented flowers last for several weeks. *Bifrenaria harrisoniae* var. *alba* is a yellow-and-white form which requires the same cultural conditions, and also flowers in spring.

Bletilla striata

This charming species is a terrestrial orchid, and can be grown in slightly shaded flowerbeds in a rich and well composted soil, which implies that they do not require additional feeding. They can also be grown in pots in a similar growing medium. *Bletilla striata* is a hardy plant, and as it is deciduous in winter and has its pseudobulbs under the soil, it can withstand low temperatures and frost. It is dormant in winter and does not require watering during this time. Flowering occurs in spring and early summer from the new seasonal growths. Plants form clumps which can easily be divided at the start of the growing season.

Brassavola cucullata

This species from South and Central America is an epiphyte and does well under intermediate conditions. It can be grown mounted on a tree or a slab of bark, and also grows well in slatted baskets with medium-size pine bark chunks. *Brassavola cucullata* has leathery terete leaves on thin pseudobulbs. It prefers high light conditions and can withstand full sun. Good humidity levels and brisk air movement are also necessary for this plant to grow and flower well. The fragrant flowers are a creamy white and appear in spring and summer. Water and feed regularly during the growing season in spring and give the plants a drier rest period in winter. Plants are hardy and will tolerate low temperatures.

Brassavola nodosa

Brassavola nodosa is from Central America and is a very hardy plant, being very similar in its requirements to *Brassavola cucullata* (on previous page), but requires a very dry winter. Although it is quite easy to grow, be careful not to overwater these plants as the sensitive roots can be damaged in this way. The numerous highly scented flowers are almost pure white and extremely attractive. Flowering occurs at various times throughout the year, but mostly in late summer and autumn.

Brassia verrucosa

Brassia verrucosa is an intermediate growing epiphyte that prefers dappled sunlight (40-50% shade). It can be grown mounted on a tree or a slab of bark, and is also very well suited to pot or basket culture. For container growing, use medium pine bark chunks (10-15 mm). This species is a very vigorous grower that forms multiple leads, and it tends to outgrow any container rapidly. Plants tolerate low temperatures well, but shelter them from frost and cold winds. Good humidity and air movement are essential, and ample watering and feeding is called for in the growing season. *Brassia verrucosa* prefers a drier winter as a rest period, so watering should be reduced to once in 7-10 days to prevent shrivelling of the pseudobulbs. The scented, spidery, green-and-white flowers occur in spring to early summer and last for about 2-3 weeks. Most *Brassia* species and their hybrids will also do well under intermediate conditions.

Calanthe vestita

Calanthe vestita is an intermediate to warm-growing terrestrial species which is deciduous in winter. These plants are best grown in shallow containers or pans in a mix of river sand and compost. They do not tolerate frost, and should be sheltered from low temperatures. They do well on patios or in an indoor sunroom, and should be grown in 40-50% shade. Good humidity and air movement are beneficial to the plants. These plants should be kept totally dry in winter once they have lost their leaves.

In late winter, flower spikes will appear from the base of the pseudobulbs, and flowers will start opening in spring. Resume watering and feeding once the new growths are visible at the base of the flowering pseudobulbs. Repotting should only be done after flowering is finished, and firm pseudobulbs should

Calanthe victoria-regina

Calanthe Sedenii Harrisii

be separated from one another and planted up singly. Plant several pseudobulbs together in a container (spaced apart to allow space for new growths), as this will provide a lovely display of flowers the following spring.

Calanthe victoria-regina is also recommended as it is easy to grow. All deciduous *Calanthe* species and their hybrids require similar conditions.

Calanthe Saint Aubin

Calanthe (Saint Aubin x Diana Broughton)

Cattleya amethystoglossa

Cattleya amethystoglossa is a robust epiphytic plant, and the pseudobulbs can reach almost a metre in height. This plant can be grown mounted, and does well in a pot with 15-20 millimetre pine bark chunks. It requires intermediate growing conditions, and likes high light levels - 30% shade is more than ample for this species. *Cattleya amethystoglossa* can tolerate low temperatures but should not be exposed to frost. Plants require ample watering and feeding in spring and summer, and should have a drier winter to rest and mature the pseudobulbs prior to flowering in spring. This species carries 8-10 large flowers in a cluster from the apex of the pseudobulb.

Cattleya aurantiaca

Cattleya aurantiaca is an intermediate-growing epiphyte that likes high light levels (30% shade). It grows well mounted or in a coarse pine bark medium, and needs regular watering and feeding in spring and summer after a drier rest period in winter. Shelter plants from frost and cold winds in winter. Flowering occurs in spring, and the numerous wax-like medium-sized flowers appear in a cluster from the apex of the pseudobulb. The flowers are mostly orange in colour, but this species can also have white, yellow or red flowers. In nature, *Cattleya aurantiaca* is often self-pollinating, and in that case the flowers do not open at all. It is best to purchase the plant either when it is in flower, or from a reputable source to avoid this problem.

Cattleya bicolor

Cattleya bicolor is an intermediate to cool-growing robust epiphytic or lithophytic plant. It can be grown mounted or trees or grown in a container with medium to large pine bark chunks. It prefers a high light intensity, with about 30% shade. It will tolerate low temperatures, but should be sheltered from frost. Regular watering and feeding in the growing season are required, with a drier rest period (water once in 7-10 days) in winter.

Regular mistings during very hot periods in summer are beneficial, as this will cool the plants and increase humidity. Brisk air movement also helps to cool the plants, as they do not like very high temperatures for long periods. 8-15 large flowers appear in spring to summer and last for 3-4 weeks.

Cattleya forbesii

Cattleya forbesii is an intermediate growing epiphyte. It is a compact but vigorous grower, normally not exceeding 25 centimetres in height. It can be grown mounted on a tree or slab of bark, and also does well in containers with medium-sized pine bark chunks. This species will tolerate low temperatures but should be sheltered from frost. High light levels with a maximum of 30% shade are adequate for this plant. Water and feed regularly in spring and summer, and reduce watering to once in 7-10 days in winter. *Cattleya forbesii* is easy to flower, and 1-5 flowers appear in spring from the apex of the mature pseudobulb.

Cattleya gaskelliana

Cattleya gaskelliana is an easy-growing epiphytic orchid suited to intermediate conditions. This species will tolerate occasional low temperatures but must be sheltered from frost. Plants do best mounted on trees or grown in baskets with medium to large pine bark chunks. *Cattleya gaskelliana* is a very vigorous grower and is not really suited to being grown in a container, as it soon outgrows the pot. It needs ample regular watering and feeding in spring and summer, and requires a cooler and drier winter, when water should only be given once in 7-10 days. This species flowers reliably in early summer, and the large (15 cm+) pink and lilac flowers are fragrant.

Cattleya intermedia

This Brazilian species is one of the easiest cattleyas to grow, and prefers intermediate conditions with high light (20-30% shade). It will tolerate full sunlight, but prefers some shading during the hottest part of the day. *Cattleya intermedia* will withstand low temperatures for short periods, and should be sheltered from frost. It is a compact grower, with the pseudobulbs rarely exceeding 30 cm in height.

This species can be grown mounted on trees or slabs of bark, and can also be grown with success in containers with medium-sized pine bark chunks. Water and feed regularly in spring and summer. Reduce watering to once in 7-10 days in winter. Flowering is from late winter to early summer, and the flower spikes appear from the apex of mature pseudobulbs. The flowers are normally in shades of pink, although alba (white) and splash-petal (peloric) varieties are also often seen.

Cattleya intermedia var. *orlata* is a very intensely coloured form, and grows under similar conditions.

Cattleya intermedia is one of the so-called cluster-type of *Cattleya* species. This group of species have long, thin pseudobulbs with 2-3 leaves at the apex. Flowers of species in this group are normally smaller in size, from 2-8 centimetres across, and mostly appear in a cluster containing 5-15 flowers. Numerous hybrids have been made which comprise species in this section, and flower colour in the hybrids range from white, green, yellow, orange and rarely pink and lilac.

Cattleya labiata

Cattleya labiata is not often found in cultivation, even though it is not difficult to grow. It prefers intermediate conditions with some protection from cold and frost. Plants do best under 30-40% shade, and although they can be mounted on trees and slabs of bark, will do very well in a container with medium-size pine bark chunks. Water and feed regularly during spring and summer, and provide a dry rest period in winter. Water should only be given every 10-14 days in winter to avoid the pseudobulbs from shrivelling. This species can flower twice a year in spring and autumn if grown well, but flowering is normally in late summer to autumn.

Cattleya labiata is the type species of the genus *Cattleya*. This species has shorter pseudobulbs, normally up to 30 centimetres, including the single leaf at the apex of the pseudobulb. Flowers are large, often 15 centimetres across, and only 2-3 appear on a flower stem. There are several species closely related to *Cattleya labiata*, and these mostly have similar cultural requirements.

Numerous *Cattleya* hybrids incorporate this species in their background, especially the large-flowered types with only 2-3 flowers. Various colour forms of this and related species are seen, from white, pink, lilac, mauve and even slate-blue, but only rarely yellow or orange. Hybrids made between the two different sections of cattleyas, namely the single-leaf types and those with 2-3 leaves, may have a large range of flower sizes, number of flowers, as well as almost any colour imaginable. These hybrids all do well under intermediate conditions.

▲ *Cattleya intermedia* var. *orlata*

◀ *Cattleya labiata*

▼ *Cattleya loddigesii*

Cattleya loddigesii and Cattleya harrisoniana

Cattleya loddigesii and *Cattleya harrisoniana* are two very similar species which grow well in intermediate conditions. They require bright light (30% shade), good humidity and ample air movement. They can be grown mounted on bark and trees, or grown in containers in medium pine bark chunks. Both require regular watering and feeding in spring and summer, with a drier resting period in winter when water should only be given once in 7-10 days. *Cattleya harrisoniana* flowers from summer into autumn, and *Cattleya loddigesii* flowers from winter into early spring. Both species have clusters of several (3 or more) large lilac to pink flowers.

Cattleya harrisoniana

Cattleya luteola

Cattleya luteola is a miniature species of the single-leaf section. Its pseudobulbs rarely exceed 15 centimetres in height, and 2-3 smallish bright yellow flowers (4-5 cm across) occur in spring. This species is an easy intermediate grower and can be grown in containers or mounted on trees or slabs of bark. Light levels of 30% shade are sufficient, and the species must be sheltered from frost, although it will tolerate occasional cold spells. Water and feed regularly in the growing season, but provide a drier rest period in winter. This serves to mature the growths prior to flowering in spring.

Cattleya maxima

Cattleya maxima is an epiphyte which grows well in intermediate conditions. It requires bright light and limited full sunlight, and will do well under 30% shading. Mount this species on a tree or slab of bark, or grow it in a container with medium to large pine bark chunks. It will tolerate some low temperatures down to 5°C, but must be sheltered from frost. Provide high humidity and good air movement. Water and feed regularly in spring and summer, but water only once in 7-10 days in winter, as *Cattleya maxima* requires a cool and dry winter rest. From 3-15 flowers appear in spring, and flowers can be up to 12 centimetres across.

▲ *Sophrolaeliocattleya* Bright Angel
 – a miniature hybrid

▶ *Laeliocattleya* Puppy Love "True Beauty"
 – a hybrid with *Laelia anceps*

▶ *Epilaeliocattleya* Don Herman "Gold Rush"

▼ *Laeliocattleya* Mini Purple "Lea" – a miniature hybrid

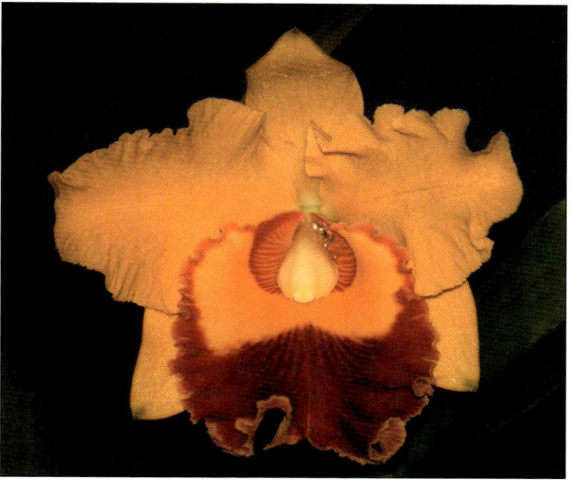

▲ *Brassolaeliocattleya* Chunyeah

◀ *Brassolaeliocattleya* Nacouchee "Mission Valley"

◀ *Brassolaeliocattleya* Alma Kee "Tip Malee"

▼ *Cattleya* Clark Herman "Carl"

Cattleya warneri

Cattleya warneri is a robust, single-leafed species which grows well under intermediate to warm conditions. It requires bright light and limited full sunlight, and will do well under 30% shade. This species can be grown mounted on a tree or piece of bark, or grow it in a container with medium to large pine bark chunks. It will tolerate some lower temperatures, but must be sheltered from frost and cold winds. Plants should be watered and fed regularly in spring and summer, but water only once in 7-10 days in winter to provide a resting period. Provide good humidity and air movement at all times. 2-5 flowers appear in spring, and these flowers can be up to 20 centimetres across.

Coelogyne cristata

Coelogyne cristata is an intermediate to cool-growing epiphyte. It does not appreciate very high temperatures in summer, but can tolerate some low temperatures in winter, provided it does not get frost. If grown in cool, shady (50-60% shade, kept below 25°C) and humid conditions with good air movement, it is a vigorous grower well-suited to basket or container culture. It requires a free-draining coarse epiphytic medium. This species should be kept moist constantly during spring and summer, with regular watering and feeding. Watering should be kept to a minimum in winter, as the roots do not like being wet and cold. Water can be given once in 10-14 days to prevent excessive shrivelling of the pseudobulbs. Flowering is in spring, and the spectacular flowers are well worth the additional effort. *Coelogyne cristata* var. *hololeuca* is a pure white form of this species which can be grown in similar conditions.

Coelogyne flaccida

Coelogyne flaccida is an extremely easy orchid to grow, as it is very hardy and tolerates low temperatures and even light frost. Plants have high light requirements and will grow in full sunlight, provided some shading is given during the hottest part of

▲ *Cattleya warneri*
◀ *Coelogyne cristata*
▼ *Coelogyne cristata* var. *hololeuca*

the day. Water and feed regularly in spring and summer, and reduce watering to once a week in winter. *Coelogyne flaccida* grows vigorously when mounted on bark or on a tree, and will quickly form a large specimen plant if grown in a container with medium pine bark chunks. Striking pendulous (hanging) flower stems bearing numerous cream-coloured flowers occur from late winter into early spring. Growers should be aware that these flowers have a sharp and unpleasant scent, and it would be advisable not to bring this species into the home when in flower.

Cuitlauzina pendula

This striking species from Mexico is an intermediate to cool epiphytic grower which is best cultivated in a pot or other container in medium to fine pine bark chunks. *Cuitlauzina pendula* does not like cold temperatures in winter and should not be exposed to temperatures below 8°C. Shading of 40-50% is recommended. Good humidity and brisk air movement are important, and during the growing season of spring and summer this species should be watered and fed regularly to keep the growing medium moist. In winter, keep this species cool and dry by only watering once in 7-10 days. Flowering occurs in late winter to early spring.

Cymbidium erythrostylum

Cymbidium erythrostylum is an intermediate to warm-growing epiphyte and semi-terrestrial which is best grown in a pot in the recommended *Cymbidium* mix. It grows well in bright light (20-30% shading) and can be grown in full sun, provided it is shaded during the hottest part of the day. Although it will tolerate some low temperatures, it should not be exposed to frost. As it is more tolerant of warmer temperatures, it does not require the cooler night temperatures that other cymbidiums do to initiate its flower spikes. Water and feed this species regularly in spring and summer, but only once a week in winter to allow a resting period. The flowering season is from late autumn until spring.

Coelogyne flaccida ▲

Cuitlauzina pendula ▶

Cymbidium erythrostylum ▼

Recommended Orchids

Cymbidium lowianum

Cymbidium lowianum

Cymbidium lowianum

Cymbidium lowianum is an intermediate-growing plant which can easily be grown outdoors in full sunlight, although plants should be sheltered from the harsh midday sun to avoid burning the leathery leaves. Cymbidiums will not flower if they do not get sufficient light. Plants are vigorous growers and gross feeders, and during the growing season of spring and summer should be watered and fed copiously. A semi-terrestrial potting mix is recommended (see Chapter 4 - *Cymbidium*). Reduce watering in winter to once a week, and resume your regular watering and feeding once the plant is in flower. Repotting should only be done after flowering when the new growths start forming. Flower stems are initiated in autumn when there is a 15°C (or more) difference between day and night temperatures. Plants grown too warm at this time may not flower. Flowering occurs in spring, and the flowers last for more than a month. The clear yellow and green variety of this species, *Cymbidium lowianum* var. *concolor*, is also often found in cultivation and grows under similar conditions.

Cymbidium lowianum var. *concolor*

Cymbidium hybrids

There are numerous *Cymbidium* hybrids freely available in the pot plant and nursery trade. All of these hybrids can be grown similar to *Cymbidium lowianum* (above). Growers must be aware that there are, however, various different types of hybrids available in this genus (see illustrations overleaf). Miniature cymbidiums have less robust growths and leaves, and have smaller flowers. Flower spikes may be erect, arching, or pendulous. Standard cymbidiums have larger but fewer flowers on large and robust plants, and flower spikes are normally erect. Intergrades between these two types are known as polymin cymbidiums, and offer medium-sized plants with a variety of flower sizes and presentation habits, dependant on the species and other hybrids in their background. Early-flowering cymbidiums are also becoming freely available. These hybrids are more tolerant of warm conditions, and as they do not depend on cold nights to initiate flower spikes, may flower from late summer onwards, and even throughout the year.

Cymbidium Nicole's Valentine - a polymin hybrid

Cymbidium Bulbarrow - a polymin hybrid

Cymbidium Tommy - a miniature hybrid

Cymbidium Winter Fire "Faultless"
- a miniature hybrid

Recommended Orchids

▲ *Cymbidium* Oakbank - a standard hybrid

▶ *Cymbidium* Strathbraan "Cooksbridge Noël"
   - a polymin hybrid

▶ *Cymbidium* Strathcoil "Oudepost Princess"
   - a standard hybrid

▼ *Cymbidium* Fancy Free "Geyserland"
   - a standard hybrid

Dendrobium bigibbum

Dendrobium bigibbum is also known as *Dendrobium phalaenopsis*. This species is an intermediate to warm grower and should not be grown at temperatures below 10°C. They are not tolerant of low temperatures and are very susceptible to frost. In cold areas they should be grown as hothouse plants, but in tropical and subtropical areas they can be grown as garden plants. Plants can become very tall and may reach up to one metre in height.

Dendrobium bigibbum is an epiphyte, and can be mounted on trees. However, it does better in small pots, as the roots prefer to be pot-bound. Use fine to medium pine bark to grow these plants. *Dendrobium bigibbum* prefers maximum sunlight, and tolerates full sun well if the humidity is high enough. High humidity and good air movement are essential to the successful cultivation of this species. Water and feed these plants throughout the year. This species and its hybrids bear numerous large, intensely-coloured flowers on long inflorescences throughout the year, but mostly in autumn and winter. Flowers can last for several months on the plant.

Dendrobium bigibbum var. *compactum*

Dendrobium bigibbum and its hybrids

The hybrids of this species and its closely related allies are numerous, and vary greatly with regard to shape and colour of the flowers. They all have similar cultural requirements. Some hybrids containing the variety *compactum* are more compact and even miniature in stature. These are easier to grow in intermediate conditions.

Dendrobium chrysotoxum

Dendrobium chrysotoxum

Dendrobium chrysotoxum is an easy intermediate-growing epiphytic plant. It can be mounted on a tree or a slab of bark, and can be grown in medium to large pine bark chunks in containers. It tolerates low temperatures for short periods, but must be sheltered from frost. Water and feed regularly in spring and summer, but reduce watering to once in 10-14 days in winter to give the plant a drier resting period. Too much water in winter will promote the formation of keikis instead of flower spikes. Average humidity and air movement, together with bright conditions (20-30% shade), will ensure success with the growing of this species. The bright yellow flowers appear in spring to early summer.

▲ *Dendrobium* King Dragon

▶ *Dendrobium* Thailand

▶ *Dendrobium* Nida "Rage"

▼ *Dendrobium* (Lady Pink x Classic Gem)

Dendrobium phalaenopsis-type hybrids

Dendrobium densiflorum

Dendrobium densiflorum is an intermediate to warm-growing epiphytic plant which will not tolerate low temperatures and frost, and which should not be grown below 8°C. Plants are nevertheless vigorous and robust and should preferably be grown mounted on a tree or a piece of bark, or in a pot or basket filled with medium to large pine bark chunks. Water and feed regularly in spring and summer, but water only once a week in winter. This species requires bright light (30% shade), but not full sunlight, as this may burn the leaves. *Dendrobium densiflorum* flowers from nodes at the top of the pseudobulbs in spring, and presents numerous bright yellow flowers on each pendulous inflorescence.

Dendrobium fimbriatum var. oculatum

Dendrobium fimbriatum is widely grown in cultivation and is regarded as an easy intermediate-growing orchid. This species should not be grown at temperatures below 5°C, and must be sheltered from frost and cold winds. Plants of this species can be very tall (pseudobulbs can be over one metre tall), and can be grown mounted on the base of trees in a shady spot (30-40% shade), or in a basket or container with fine to medium pine bark chips. Watering and feeding should be done throughout spring and summer, but as the plants require a resting period in winter, water should only be given once in 7-10 days. This species flowers in spring. The clear yellow-flowered *Dendrobium fimbriatum* is fairly rare in cultivation, but the variety *oculatum* which has a dark maroon blotch at the base of the lip, is often seen and easy to obtain.

Dendrobium kingianum

This charming species is from Australia, where it is immensely variable in flower colour and growth size, and can be found growing as an epiphyte or a lithophyte. It will tolerate full sunlight, but should best be grown with about 20% shading.

Dendrobium densiflorum ▲
Dendrobium fimbriatum var. *oculatum* ▶
Dendrobium kingianum - a pale pink form ▼

Dendrobium Rutherford's Blushing Bride

Dendrobium Jesmond Glitter

Dendrobium Yondi Gold

Dendrobium Gillieston Jazz

It can be mounted on a tree or slab of bark, and also in a container with fine pine bark chips. An addition of marble chips to the growing medium is often beneficial, and helps to anchor the plant in its container. This species can even be grown on large rocks in the garden. Plants can tolerate low temperatures and light frost, but do best if sheltered from very low temperatures.

Dendrobium kingianum requires average humidity, but brisk air movement is essential to good culture of these plants, as the breeze helps to cool them, especially those grown in full sunlight. Watering and feeding must be done regularly in the growing season, but plants prefer to be cool and dry in winter when they are essentially dormant. Light watering once in 10-14 days will prevent excessive shrivelling of the pseudobulbs. Too much water in winter will inhibit flowering in spring, and may promote the formation of keikis instead of flowers.

Dendrobium kingianum is found in the background of numerous hybrids of related species. These hybrids are often referred to as the Australian dendrobiums, or the *kingianum*-type hybrids. The cultural requirements of these hybrids are the same as for *Dendrobium kingianum*, and they are easy to grow and flower as garden plants in South Africa.

Dendrobium kingianum – a dark mauve form which has resulted from selective breeding

Dendrobium moschatum

Dendrobium moschatum is an easy-growing orchid requiring intermediate conditions. This species should not be grown at temperatures below 5°C, and must be sheltered from frost and cold winds. Plants of this species can be very tall (pseudobulbs can be over one metre tall), and can be mounted on the base of trees in a shady spot (30-40% shade), or in a basket or container with fine to medium pine bark chips. Watering and feeding should be done regularly throughout the year, but as the plants require a resting period in winter, water should only be given once in 7-10 days. Too much water in winter may promote the formation of keikis along the mature pseudobulb, and plants forming keikis may not flower at all. This species flowers in spring. The flowers of *Dendrobium moschatum* are unusual in that the lip is not flat, but in the shape of a pouch.

Dendrobium moschatum

Dendrobium nobile

Dendrobium nobile is a very easy intermediate-growing species. Plants are vigorous and are best grown mounted, or potted in medium (10-15 mm) pine bark chips. This species is especially suited to being mounted on the side of a tree trunk where it can get full sunlight, provided it gets some shelter from the hot midday sun. It can also be grown on deciduous trees, as it requires full sunlight in winter to mature the pseudobulbs in order to promote maximum flowering in spring. This species will tolerate low temperatures to 2°C for short periods, but the soft leaves are susceptible to damage from frost.

Water and feed this species copiously in the growing season, but withhold water almost entirely from late autumn onwards until spring. At most, it is recommended that *Dendrobium nobile* should only receive light watering once in 14-21 days in winter, and then only if the pseudobulbs appear to be shrivelling a lot. Flower buds appear in late winter along nodes on the pseudobulbs, but will rather form keikis or plantlets if watered too soon. The grower should only resume watering and feeding the plant after the flower buds are clearly discernible as buds. The plants flower in spring, and flowers last for 3-4 weeks.

Dendrobium nobile

Dendrobium nobile var. *virginale*

A pure white variety of *Dendrobium nobile*, namely *Dendrobium nobile* var. *virginale* is also found in cultivation. This variety has the same cultural requirements as *Dendrobium nobile*, but will not tolerate having its roots disturbed, and should only be repotted when absolutely necessary.

Dendrobium nobile hybrids

There are numerous hybrids available which have *Dendrobium nobile* and *Dendrobium nobile* var. *virginale* in their background. These plants are also sometimes referred to as the Yamamoto dendrobiums, so named after a Mr Yamamoto who originally worked on this breeding line. All of these hybrids have the same cultural requirements as *Dendrobium nobile* (above), and should be grown in the same way. There are numerous different colours and shapes of flowers available in this breeding line.

Dendrobium Prima Donna

Dendrobium Sakura "Hine" - a miniature hybrid which grows vigorously

Dendrobium Orange Gem

Dendrobium Pittero Gold "Grace"

Recommended Orchids

Dendrobium speciosum

Dendrobium speciosum is another Australian species which is found as an epiphyte and a lithophyte. This species is large and robust, and the thick pseudobulbs with flower stems can exceed one and a half metres in height. It is very hardy and grows in full sunlight, and can withstand low temperatures as well as light frost. As this species is so large, it should best be grown at the base of a tree, mounted on a large piece of bark, or even on a large rock as a rockery plant. *Dendrobium speciosum* can also be grown in containers, but these must be suitably large and quite sturdy to accommodate mature plants. Large pine bark chunks with some marble chips added in make a suitable potting medium.

This species requires good humidity and air movement, and can be watered and fed copiously in the growing season. In winter, this plant has a resting period when water should only be given once in every 7-10 days. There are several named varieties of this species with variable plant sizes. *Dendrobium speciosum* is also often used in hybridising (see *Dendrobium kingianum* on page 71) and its hybrids and varieties all have similar cultural requirements. It produces a large number of medium-sized cream-coloured flowers per spike, and flowers in late spring to early summer.

Dendrobium speciosum

Dendrobium tetragonum

Dendrobium tetragonum

Dendrobium tetragonum also originates from Australia and is often used in the breeding of the Australian dendrobiums. The large, spidery flowers with their unusual colours are most attractive, and pseudobulbs are rectangular in cross-section.

Dendrobium tetragonum is an intermediate-growing epiphyte which grows well when mounted on bark or on a tree trunk. The pseudobulbs are club-like and swell toward the apex, sometimes making the plant top-heavy. For this reason it is best only grown in stable containers, or those containing ample crocks to anchor the pot. Grow this species in fine to medium pine bark chunks. It can tolerate occasional cold spells, but must be sheltered from frost. Bright but dappled sunlight (20-30% shade), combined with good humidity and brisk air movement contribute to the successful cultivation of this species. Water and feed often in the growing season, with a drier and cooler resting period in winter when the plant should only be watered sparingly. Flowers occur in spring.

Dendrobium thyrsiflorum

Dendrobium thyrsiflorum is an intermediate to warm-growing epiphytic plant which will not tolerate low temperatures and frost, and which should not be grown below 8°C. Plants are nevertheless vigorous and robust, and should preferably be grown mounted on a tree or a piece of bark, or can be grown in a pot or basket filled with medium to large pine bark chunks. This species easily forms large specimen plants, and does not like to have its roots disturbed. When planted in a container, ensure to use one that will allow several years of unhindered growth.

Water and feed regularly in spring and summer, but water only once a week in winter. This species requires bright light (30% shade), but not full sunlight, as this may burn the leaves. *Dendrobium thyrsiflorum* flowers from nodes at the top of the pseudobulbs in spring, and presents numerous orange and white flowers on each pendulous inflorescence. A well-grown and flowered large plant is an awesome sight to behold.

Encyclia fragrans

Encyclia fragrans is an easy-growing intermediate epiphyte which has been in cultivation since 1787. This species is a vigorous grower which easily forms large specimen plants. It requires bright to shady conditions (40-50% shade) and can be watered and fed throughout the year. *Encyclia fragrans* can be mounted on a tree or slab of bark, but also does well in a container with medium size pine bark chunks. This species flowers in spring, and the cream-coloured flowers are fragrant.

Encyclia prismatocarpa

Encyclia prismatocarpa is a vigorous and hardy epiphyte which does well under intermediate conditions. This species easily forms large specimen plants and will tolerate full sunlight, provided it receives some shading during the hottest part of the day. Plants will do best under 20-30% shade. They can be mounted on a tree or a piece of bark, and can be grown in a basket or container in medium-sized pine bark chunks. Due to its vigorous growth habit, growers must choose a container that will provide for several years' growth. Feed and water regularly throughout the year. The long-lasting and brightly-coloured flowers appear from spring till summer.

This species may also be known as *Prosthechea prismatocarpa*, as well as *Hormidium prismatocarpum*.

Epidendrum radicans

This commonly grown reed-stem *Epidendrum* species is an epiphyte, but also grows semi-terrestrially, often forming large clumps, which produce their bright orange flowers from the apex of mature growths throughout the year. It can be grown in containers with a fine to medium pine bark mix, and also as a garden plant in flowerbeds with sandy, compost-rich soil. This species produces roots all along its erect stems, and can be grown with success at the base of a tree, which may provide additional support for the growths. *Epidendrum radicans* grows in full sun and can be watered and fed throughout the year. It will tolerate low temperatures, but should be sheltered from frost.

Epidendrum secundum and its hybrids

This species is a reed-stem *Epidendrum*, which can be grown in containers or in flowerbeds in sandy compost-rich soil. *Epidendrum secundum* and its hybrids occur in a vast range of colours, including white, pink, mauve, lilac, yellow, orange and red. These plants are commonly called the "poor man's orchid" since they grow vigorously, produce numerous keikis on old flower stems, and are easy to care for. They grow in full sun and flower throughout the year from the apex of mature growths. Plants can be watered and fed throughout the year for the best results, and will tolerate occasional low temperatures. Although the plants should be sheltered from frost, they are nevertheless grown in gardens throughout South Africa.

Goodyera daibuzanensis

Goodyera daibuzanensis is a low-growing terrestrial which thrives under intermediate to warm conditions. This species requires low light levels and does best in conditions of 60-70% shade. It does not tolerate cold or frost and must be grown above 10°C. In tropical and subtropical areas, it can be grown outside as a pot plant, but in colder climates it must receive warmth and shelter. Plant this species in equal parts river sand and commercial potting soil in shallow pans. Provide good humidity and air movement, with regular watering and feeding throughout the year. *Goodyera daibuzanensis* is a "jewel" orchid which is grown for the beauty of its attractively marked leaves, and not for its insignificant flowers.

Laelia anceps

Laelia anceps is a very hardy intermediate-growing plant which can grow in full sun or light shade (20% shading), and can tolerate low temperatures and even light frost. It should be watered and fed regularly in spring and summer, but requires a cool and dry winter to mature the pseudobulbs. Flowers occur on tall, erect inflorescences from late winter to spring. This plant is an epiphyte, and can easily be grown on trees, mounted on bark, or attached to a rock in a sunny and bright position. Average humidity and good air movement are beneficial to successful culture of this attractive species. There are several different colour forms, e.g. *Laelia anceps* var. *veitchiana*.

Laelia anceps is closely related to the *Cattleya* alliance, and numerous intergeneric hybrids contain this species in their background. Hybrids with *Laelia anceps* in their background are easy to grow, and flower well.

Laelia crispa

Laelia crispa is a robust *Cattleya*-like plant which does well under intermediate conditions, and grows well mounted on a tree, a piece of bark or in a container with medium to large pine bark chunks. This species likes high light levels, and should be given shading of at most 30% in order to grow and flower well. Water and feed regularly in spring and summer, but reduce watering to once in 7-10 days in winter to allow the plant a resting period during which the pseudobulbs can mature. This species will tolerate some low temperatures, but should not be exposed to frost. The *Cattleya*-like flowers (over 10 cm across) appear in spring on an erect inflorescence.

Laelia anceps ▲
Laelia anceps var. *veitchiana* ▶
Laelia crispa ▼

Laelia flava

Laelia flava is a rupicolous or rock-growing species from Brazil which requires intermediate conditions. It is a hardy plant, and while it grows among grasses and other sparse vegetation, it is often exposed to full sunlight.

Plants can tolerate heat and cold equally well, and will survive a mild frost. Grow these plants on the rocks in a rockery, or in a pot with equal parts of fine pine bark chunks and marble chips. Provide a maximum of 20% shade, and water and feed up to twice a week in spring and summer. Give water sparingly once every two weeks in winter, as the plants are dormant in the cooler months. *Laelia flava* grows in very harsh conditions in nature, and will not produce its yellow flowers in cultivation if its requirements are not met.

Laelia milleri is another rupicolous species with similar cultural requirements, and has orange-red flowers. These species flower in spring.

▲ *Laelia flava*
◀ *Laelia milleri*
▼ *Laelia lundii*

Laelia lundii

Laelia lundii is a miniature species which grows best under intermediate conditions, but which can tolerate occasional cold spells and even light frost, as it is quite hardy. Plants tolerate bright to full sun, but it is best to provide 20% shading to protect the leaves from burning. It has a creeping habit and is best grown mounted on bark or on a tree in a sunny position. Watering and feeding can be given throughout the year, and flowers appear in late winter to spring.

Laelia purpurata

Laelia purpurata

Laelia purpurata is a robust *Cattleya*-like plant which thrives under intermediate conditions, and grows well mounted on a tree, a piece of bark or in a container with medium to large pine bark chunks. This species likes high light levels, and should be given shading of at most 30% in order to grow and flower well. Water and feed regularly in spring and summer, but reduce watering to once in 7-10 days in winter to allow the plant a resting period during which the pseudobulbs can mature. *Laelia purpurata* will tolerate some low temperatures, but should not be exposed to frost. The large *Cattleya*-like flowers (over 15 cm across) appear from early to midsummer. Various colour forms are available.

Laelia purpurata var. *werckhauseri* – a slate blue colour form

Laeliocattleya Gold Digger "Buttercup"
– a cluster type hybrid

Sophrolaeliocattleya Coastal Sunrise "Pink Surprise"

Some *Cattleya* alliance hybrids

Potinara Little Toshie "Gold Country"
– a miniature hybrid

Cattleya Horace "Maxima"

Ludisia discolor

Ludisia discolor is an intermediate to warm-growing terrestrial. It occurs in nature on forest floors in shady, humid and warm areas. Grow this species in shallow containers in a mix of equal parts of river sand and commercial potting soil. It should be grown under 70-80% shade, with high humidity and good air movement. Water and feed regularly throughout the year, and ensure that the potting medium remains evenly moist, never drying out completely between waterings. This plant is intolerant of cold and frost, and should be grown at temperatures above 10°C. *Ludisia discolor* is commonly known as a "jewel" orchid. It has attractive yellow-veined dark maroon leaves, and is normally grown as a specimen plant to show off the foliage. The somewhat uninteresting flowers are of lesser importance to the orchid grower.

▲ *Ludisia discolor* - flowers
◀ *Ludisia discolor* - plant with velvety, yellow-veined leaves
▼ *Maxillaria picta*

Maxillaria picta

Maxillaria picta is a compact-growing epiphyte which grows easily under intermediate conditions. It can be mounted on a tree or slab of bark, and also grows well in containers with fine to medium pine bark chunks. It will tolerate low temperatures, but must be sheltered from frost. Grow this plant in bright dappled sunlight (30-40% shading), and feed and water regularly throughout the year. *Maxillaria picta* flowers in spring, and the flowers have a sweet fragrance.

Maxillaria variabilis

Maxillaria variabilis is a plant with a miniature growth habit, and is an epiphyte or lithophyte which grows easily under intermediate conditions, often forming large specimen plants. It can be grown mounted on bark or on a tree, and also does well in a container or basket with fine to medium pine bark chunks. Plants prefer dappled sunlight or shading of 30-40%, and although they will tolerate some low temperatures, should be sheltered from frost. Watering and feeding can take place throughout the year, and vigorous plants can almost permanently be in flower, although flowering is predominantly in spring and summer. Flowers vary from yellow to red in colour.

Miltonia clowesii

Miltonia clowesii is an intermediate to warm-growing epiphyte which does very well in South African climatic conditions. This species grows well either mounted on bark or on a tree, and does equally well in containers with fine to medium-sized pine bark chunks. Dappled sunlight or shading at 30-40% is optimal. Good humidity levels and brisk air movement are also beneficial to the successful culture of this species. Water and feed regularly throughout the year. Although *Miltonia clowesii* does tolerate the occasional cold spell, it should be sheltered from frost. Flowering occurs from late winter to early summer, and because the flowers open sequentially on the flower stem, plants can be in flower for a month or more.

Miltonia flavescens

Miltonia flavescens is an easy-growing, vigorous epiphyte which often forms large specimen plants. Plants can be mounted on bark slabs or tree branches, or may be grown in containers with fine to medium-sized pine bark chunks. Bright light with slight (20%) shading produces the best growth, with good humidity and air movement contributing to its vigour. *Miltonia flavescens* will tolerate some low temperatures, but the soft leaves are vulnerable to frost and cold winds. Water and feed regularly throughout the year. Flowers appear in early to midsummer, when 15-20 starry cream-coloured flowers all open at the same time on an erect flower spike. Flowers last for 2-3 weeks, and have a slightly sweet scent.

Miltonia regnellii

Miltonia regnellii is an intermediate-growing epiphytic plant. It may be mounted on a tree or a piece of bark, and also grows well in containers with fine to medium-sized pine bark chunks. This species requires some shading from full sun and does best under 30-40% shade. Although it does not tolerate frost, it will withstand the occasional cold spell to 5°C. Water and feed regularly throughout the year, and provide good humidity and air movement. Flowering occurs from spring to summer.

Miltonia spectabilis

Miltonia spectabilis is an intermediate to warm-growing epiphytic plant which can be mounted on bark or on a tree, or which can successfully be grown in containers with fine to medium-sized pine bark chunks. This species will tolerate low temperatures, but should not be exposed to frost or temperatures below 5°C. Plants require good humidity and air movement, and should be grown under 30-40% shading. *Miltonia spectabilis* is a vigorous grower which readily forms large specimen plants which are a sight to behold when in flower during spring. The flowers have cream-coloured sepals and petals with a pink lip. Water and feed regularly throughout the year for the best results.

A dark mauve variety of this species has recently been granted species status and is known as *Miltonia moreliana*. *Miltonia moreliana* has the same cultural requirements as *Miltonia spectabilis*, but is not such a vigorous grower and does not form large plants quickly. In cooler areas, grow this species under shadier conditions (40-50%) and at temperatures above 10°C, and shelter plants from cold winds. Other recommended varieties of this species are: *Miltonia spectabilis* var. *roseum*, and *Miltonia spectabilis* var. *alba*.

Miltonia regnellii ▲
Miltonia spectabilis ▶
Miltonia moreliana ▼

Miltonia spectabilis var. *roseum*

Miltonia spectabilis var. *alba*

Miltassia Explorer
- easy intermediate growing hybrid

Vuylstekeara Violet Wood
- an intermediate to warm growing hybrid

Maclellanara Pagan Love Song "Ruby Charles" - intermediate to cool growing

Neofinetia falcata

Neofinetia falcata is a charming miniature epiphytic species in the *Vanda* alliance, with which it breeds readily to form equally charming hybrids. It grows well under intermediate to cool conditions, and is best grown mounted on a tree or piece of bark, or in a container with fine to medium pine bark chunks. Grow this plant under conditions of 20-30% shade, and try to avoid exposure to temperatures above 30°C. Provide high humidity and good air movement, and mist the plant regularly on very hot days. *Neofinetia falcata* tolerates cold weather well, and can withstand light frost. Water and feed copiously in spring and summer, but sparingly, once in 10-14 days, during winter as this species requires a resting period. Flowering normally occurs in spring and summer, and the flowers have a pleasant fragrance.

Neofinetia falcata

Oncidium flexuosum

Oncidium flexuosum is one of numerous *Oncidium* species which grow well under intermediate conditions. It is an epiphyte, but as it has a vigorous, rambling and spreading growth habit, mature plants are not well suited to being grown in containers. These plants are best grown in baskets with medium-sized pine bark chunks, or mounted on trees or large pieces of bark. This species grows well in a semi-shaded position, with 30-40% shading. Provide good humidity and brisk air movement, and water and feed regularly throughout the year. Whilst this species will withstand some low temperatures, it does not tolerate frost. Flowers occur from spring until summer on long, branched inflorescences.

Oncidium flexuosum has been used extensively in the breeding of *Oncidium* hybrids and numerous related intergeneric hybrids. It imparts its vigour and ease of culture to these hybrids, even though many of the other species used in breeding intergeneric hybrids are cool-growing plants.

Oncidium flexuosum

Oncidium ornithorhynchum

Oncidium ornithorhynchum is a compact, intermediate to cool-growing epiphytic species which can be grown mounted on a tree or piece of bark. Plants do well in containers with fine to medium-sized pine bark chunks. It prefers to be kept cool and slightly shady (40-50% shade) and dislikes temperatures above 30°C for long periods of time. Plants will tolerate some cold temperatures, but should be sheltered from frost. Provide high humidity and brisk air movement all year round, as this will also assist to keep the plant cool. Feed and water regularly (keeping the roots evenly moist) from spring until the end of the flowering season in mid-winter. After the sharply-scented flowers have dropped from the spike, give the plant a dry resting period (water lightly once in 7-10 days) until the new growths can be seen emerging from its base. When the new growths emerge, regular watering and feeding can start again.

Oncidium ornithorhynchum is also often used in hybridising and is used for its pink colour and scent, the latter becoming more muted and pleasant in its offspring.

Oncidium ornithorhynchum

Oncidium sarcodes

Oncidium sarcodes

Oncidium sarcodes is an epiphytic species which grows well in intermediate conditions. It can be grown under bright, but dappled sunlight (30-40% shade), and while it can tolerate some low temperatures, should not be exposed to frost. Grow this species mounted on a tree or on a piece of bark, or in a container with medium-sized pine bark chunks. Provide good humidity and air movement, with regular watering and feeding throughout the year. *Oncidium sarcodes* flowers in spring, but even though it is a compact plant under 30 centimetres tall, the arching inflorescence carrying numerous 5 centimetre wide flowers can be over one metre long.

Oncidium sphacelatum

Oncidium sphacelatum is a vigorous epiphytic species that does well under intermediate conditions. It is a very hardy orchid and can withstand great fluctuations in temperature from 2-35°C. It grows well in full sun, or with slight (10-20%) shading. It quickly forms large specimen plants and is not really well suited to being grown in containers, as it will quickly outgrow them. It can however be grown in containers while the plant is still small, and should be potted in medium to large pine bark chunks. *Oncidium sphacelatum* does best when mounted on a tree or piece of bark, and can also be grown on rocks or tree trunks in a rockery. Grow these plants in full sun, water and feed copiously throughout the year, provide good humidity and air movement and stand back and prepare to be amazed. The profusion of literally thousands of flowers on large, well-grown plants in spring will take your breath away.

Oncidium sphacelatum is also used in hybridising, as this species imparts its vigorous and easy growth habit and long branching inflorescences.

Oncidium sphacelatum

Oncidium Nancy

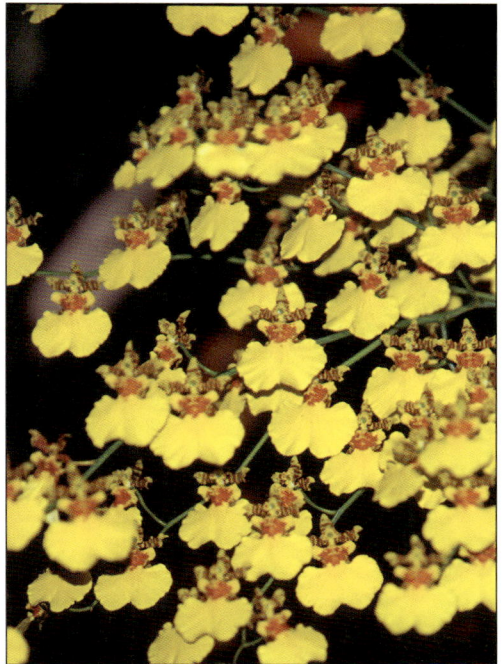

Oncidium Gower Ramsey "Volcano Queen"

Oncidium Sharry Baby "Sweet Fragrance" - highly fragrant and easy to grow

Odontocidium Artur Elle

Recommended Orchids

Paphiopedilum callosum

Paphiopedilum callosum is an intermediate to warm-growing semi-terrestrial species, which should be grown in a container with the recommended mix for paphiopedilums (Chapter 4), being two parts fine or seedling grade pine bark chips and one part marble chips.

This species has dark-green mottled leaves and is intolerant of cold, and should be grown at temperatures above 12°C. In colder climates, these plants should be grown indoors or in heated greenhouses to protect them from frost. Water must be given regularly throughout the year to ensure that the potting medium always remains evenly moist, and feed regularly with half-strength liquid fertiliser. Good humidity and air movement are also important. *Paphiopedilum callosum* is a low-light plant. Grow this species and its numerous hybrids in conditions of 60-70% shade. Flowering is from autumn to winter and spring.

Paphiopedilum concolor

Paphiopedilum concolor is a lithophytic species which occurs on limestone rocks in nature. Although this group of limestone-growing slipper orchids are the most difficult to maintain in cultivation, *Paphiopedilum concolor* is much more forgiving and will grow and flower in regular *Paphiopedilum* mix in containers. Grow this species under 30-40% shade but ensure high humidity and brisk air movement. Regular watering and feeding with half-strength liquid fertiliser should be given in spring and summer, but only water once a week in the cooler winter months. *Paphiopedilum concolor* will tolerate temperatures down to 5°C and even lower for short periods, but must be sheltered from frost. Flowering occurs from winter to early spring.

Paphiopedilum delenatii

Paphiopedilum delenatii is an intermediate to warm-growing semi-terrestrial species, which should be grown in a container with the recommended mix for paphiopedilums.

This species has dark-green mottled leaves and is intolerant of cold, and should be grown at temperatures above 12°C. In colder climates, these plants should be grown indoors or in heated greenhouses to protect them from frost. Water must be given regularly throughout the year to ensure that the potting medium always remains evenly moist, and feed regularly with half-strength liquid fertiliser. Good humidity and brisk air movement are important to grow this plant well. *Paphiopedilum delenatii* likes fairly bright light and will grow and flower well under 40-50% shade, with flowering from spring till early summer.

Paphiopedilum hirsutissimum

Paphiopedilum hirsutissimum is an intermediate to cool-growing semi-terrestrial species, which is best grown in containers with *Paphiopedilum* mix. This species with its clear green leaves should be kept evenly moist in spring and summer with regular watering and feeding with half-strength liquid fertiliser, but can be given a drier rest in the cooler months when water should only be applied once a week. Grow these plants under shading of 40-50%. *Paphiopedilum hirsutissimum* can tolerate temperatures down to 5°C, but must be sheltered from frost. Good humidity and air movement assist in the successful culture of this species. Flowering occurs in spring.

Paphiopedilum hirsutissimum

Paphiopedilum insigne

Paphiopedilum insigne is an intermediate to cool-growing semi-terrestrial species, which is best grown in containers with *Paphiopedilum* mix. In tropical and subtropical areas, this species can be grown in flower beds with sandy soil rich in compost, with the flowerbeds situated under shady trees. This species with its clear green leaves should be kept evenly moist in spring and summer with regular watering and feeding with half-strength liquid fertiliser, but can be given a drier rest in the cooler months when water should only be applied once a week. Grow these plants under shading of 40-50%. *Paphiopedilum insigne* can tolerate temperatures down to 5°C, but must be sheltered from frost. This species is in the background of numerous complex hybrids, which have similar cultural requirements. *Paphiopedilum insigne* flowers from late autumn, through winter into spring.

Paphiopedilum insigne

Paphiopedilum micranthum

Paphiopedilum micranthum is one of a group of species discovered in the last two decades in South-western China. These species grow in harsh conditions on exposed cliff faces where they are subjected to full sunlight, little regular rainfall and strong winds. Most of these species are considered difficult to maintain and flower in cultivation, but *Paphiopedilum micranthum* is the exception.

Grow *Paphiopedilum micranthum* in a shallow container with recommended *Paphiopedilum* mix, and water and feed with half-strength liquid fertiliser no more than twice a week in spring and summer. Reduce watering to once in 10-14 days in winter. Plants grow best in almost full sunlight, with at most 30% shading. Average humidity is beneficial, but brisk to strong air movement is essential all year round to ensure the health and flowering of this species. Keep plants in intermediate conditions, but although they will tolerate low temperatures, shelter them from frost. The hybrids made from species in this new section are luckily much easier to grow and flower in cultivation.

Paphiopedilum micranthum flowers from spring into summer.

Paphiopedilum micranthum "Christian"

Paphiopedilum parishii "Wiaan"

Paphiopedilum parishii

Paphiopedilum parishii is a green-leaved epiphyte which grows well under intermediate conditions. This species can be grown mounted, but as the roots of the plant may dry out too much when mounted, it is best grown in a container with fine to medium pine bark chips. *Paphiopedilum parishii* tolerates low temperatures, but must be sheltered from frost. Water and feed with half-strength liquid fertiliser regularly throughout the year, and provide good humidity and air movement. This species does best in shading of 40-50%, and produces an arching flower spike with 8-10 large green and brown flowers from late winter into spring.

Paphiopedilum sukhakulii

Paphiopedilum sukhakulii

Paphiopedilum sukhakulii is an intermediate to warm-growing semi-terrestrial species, which should be grown in a container with the recommended mix for paphiopedilums.

This species has dark-green mottled leaves and is intolerant of cold, and should be grown at temperatures above 12°C. In colder climates, these plants should be grown indoors or in heated greenhouses to protect them from frost. Water must be given regularly throughout the year to ensure that the potting medium always remains evenly moist, and feed regularly with half-strength liquid fertiliser. Good humidity and air movement are also important. *Paphiopedilum sukhakulii* requires conditions of 60-70% shade, and is frequently used in hybridising. Flowering occurs from late winter into spring.

Paphiopedilum villosum

Paphiopedilum villosum is an intermediate to cool-growing semi-terrestrial species, which is best grown in containers with *Paphiopedilum* mix. This species with its clear green leaves should be kept evenly moist in spring and summer with regular watering and feeding with half-strength liquid fertiliser, but can be given a drier rest in the cooler months when water should only be applied once a week. Grow these plants under shading of 40-50%. *Paphiopedilum villosum* can tolerate occasional low temperatures down to 5°C, but must be sheltered from frost. Good humidity and air movement must be provided. This species is also often used in hybridising, and flowers in winter to spring.

Paphiopedilum villosum

Paphiopedilum Macabre
- a mottled-leaf hybrid requiring some warmth

Paphiopedilum Vintner's Treasure "Rage"
- a mottled-leaf hybrid

Paphiopedilum Maudiae "The Queen"
- a mottled-leaf hybrid

Paphiopedilum Armeni White
- a hybrid of two Chinese species

Paphiopedilum Tommie Hanes "Williamdale"

Paphiopedilum British Bulldog "Rage"

Green-leafed hybrids

Paphiopedilum Carmen Coll

Paphiopedilum Inca "Robe"

Phalaenopsis amabilis

Phalaenopsis amabilis is a warm-growing epiphytic species. This species should be grown in a container with medium-sized pine bark chips, and must be given 60-70% shading throughout the year. High humidity and good air movement are of paramount importance in growing this plant successfully. Water and feed regularly throughout the year. Grow this species under warm conditions, and do not expose plants to temperatures below 12°C, and definitely shelter this plant from cold and frost. It is recommended that *Phalaenopsis amabilis* and all *Phalaenopsis* hybrids be grown indoors throughout the year. They flower from late winter into spring and early summer.

Other species which have similar cultural requirements to *Phalaenopsis amabilis* include *Phalaenopsis equestris, Phalaenopsis lueddemanniana, Phalaenopsis schilleriana, Phalaenopsis stuartiana,* and *Phalaenopsis violacea.* These species flower at various times throughout the year, but mostly from winter to early summer.

Phalaenopsis amabilis

Phalaenopsis equestris

Phalaenopsis lueddemanniana

Phalaenopsis schilleriana

Phalaenopsis stuartiana

Phalaenopsis violacea

Phalaenopsis Michael Tibbs - a multi-floral hybrid

Phalaenopsis lindenii

Phalaenopsis lindenii is an intermediate to cool-growing epiphytic species, and can be difficult to maintain in cultivation if grown too warm. This species should be grown in a container with medium-sized pine bark chips, and must be given 50-60% shading throughout the year. *Phalaenopsis lindenii* is one of very few *Phalaenopsis* species which can be grown mounted. High humidity and good air movement are of paramount importance in growing this plant successfully. Water and feed copiously throughout the year. Grow this species as cool as possible, with a maximum recommended temperature of 25°C in summer. Although cooler growing, *Phalaenopsis lindenii* will not tolerate frost.

Phalaenopsis Flor de Niebla

Phalaenopsis lindenii

Phalaenopsis Dou-dii Girl

Phalaenopsis Red Thrill

Phalaenopsis Ever-spring King

Phalaenopsis Hatsuyuki

Phalaenopsis Taipei Gold

Phalaenopsis Judy Freed

Phalaenopsis Bonnie Vasquez "Zuma Canyon"

Phaius tankervilleae

Phaius tankervilleae is an intermediate-growing terrestrial species which does well in flowerbeds with sandy, richly composted soil, or when grown in containers in a mix of equal parts of river sand and commercial potting soil. The robust plants grow vigorously and quickly fill containers that are not large enough to accommodate them. This species occurs in swampy areas in nature, and must be watered copiously in spring and summer.

Plants can be given additional fertiliser, but this should not be necessary if the soil contains sufficient compost. Provide a dry resting period in winter when this species is dormant and only requires light watering once in 10-14 days. *Phaius tankervilleae* can be grown in full sun and does not require shading, provided it is grown wet enough and with ample air movement. The metre-long flower spikes appear in spring, and carry numerous large long-lasting flowers.

The white and green form of this species, *Phaius tankervilleae* var. *alba* is also often seen in cultivation and grows under similar conditions, although it does benefit from at most 30% shade during summer.

Phaius tankervillae ▲

Phaius tankervilleae var. *alba* ▼

Renanthera imschootiana

Renanthera imschootiana is a warm-growing epiphyte with leathery leaves which can tolerate full sun. It can be grown mounted on a tree or piece of bark, or can be grown in a container with large pine bark chunks. Plants should be watered and fed regularly throughout the year. They require high humidity and good air movement to do well. This species does not tolerate frost or constant cold temperatures below 10°C, and should be sheltered in winter in the colder areas of the country. It flowers in summer.

Renanthera monachica is a species with similar cultural requirements, and flowers from spring until summer.

▲ *Renanthera imschootiana*
◄ *Renanthera monachica*
▼ *Schomburgkia tibicinis*

Schomburgkia tibicinis

Schomburgkia tibicinis is a robust, easy-growing epiphytic species which does well under intermediate conditions. This species can be grown in full sun or semi-shade, and is well suited to being mounted on trees, grown on rocks in the garden, or grown in a container or basket with large pine bark chunks. *Schomburgkia tibicinis* is extremely hardy and will withstand high summer temperatures and even light frost in winter. It should be watered and fed regularly in spring and summer, but as plants are dormant in winter, *Schomburgkia tibicinis* should only be given light watering once in 10-14 days. This plant produces a metre-long inflorescence carrying a cluster of 8-10 centimetre wide flowers in spring.

Sobralia macrantha

Sobralia macrantha is a tall-growing reed-like terrestrial which grows well in intermediate conditions in richly composted soil in flowerbeds, or in containers in commercial potting soil. Plants can be grown in full sun, and must be watered regularly in spring and summer. This species has a resting period in winter, and should only be watered once in 7-10 days during this season. The large flowers appear in early summer and only last for 2-3 days, but several flowers are produced from the apex of the growths over a period of 3-4 weeks, ensuring a constant display on large plants.

Sobralia macrantha ▲

Stanhopea connata ▶

Stanhopea oculata ▼

Stanhopea wardii

Stanhopea wardii is an intermediate-growing epiphyte with large leathery leaves which can withstand full sun. Shading at 20-30% will however prevent the leaves from being burnt, and is recommended. This species must be grown mounted on a tree branch or grown in a basket in large pine bark chunks, as the wax-like highly scented flowers grow downward and hang below the plant. Water and feed this species regularly in spring and summer, but only once in 10-14 days in winter as the plants have a dormant resting period. Plants grow vigorously and form large specimens which produce several short-lived flowers (5-7 days) in late summer. Other species which have similar cultural requirements include *Stanhopea oculata*, which flowers in mid-summer, and *Stanhopea connata*, which flowers from summer to autumn.

Stanhopea wardii

Vanda coerulea

Vanda coerulea is an intermediate to cool-growing epiphyte. This species can be mounted on a tree or piece of bark, or grown in a container with large pine bark chunks. Good humidity and air movement are beneficial to it, and it will withstand temperatures down to 5°C, but must be sheltered from frost. This species should be grown indoors or under cover in winter in colder areas of the country. Water and feed regularly throughout the year. Grow plants in bright dappled sunlight with 30-40% shading. *Vanda coerulea* flowers from autumn to early winter.

Vanda coerulea
- growing on a tree in Pietermaritzburg

Vanda luzonica

Vanda luzonica is an intermediate to warm-growing epiphyte. This robust species may be grown at the base of trees in 30-40% shade in the tropical and subtropical areas of South Africa, but should be grown under shelter in the colder areas of the country during winter. Plants do not tolerate low temperatures below 8°C and must be protected from frost. High humidity and good air movement are essential, and watering and feeding must be done regularly throughout the year. *Vanda luzonica* flowers in spring.

Vanda Miss Joaquim

Vanda Miss Joaquim is a primary hybrid between the species *Vanda hookeriana* and *Vanda teres*. This hybrid has been in cultivation since 1893. The hybrid and the species are terete-leaved epiphytes which are best grown as garden plants as they can become very tall. They tolerate full sun, but require high humidity and good air movement to flourish. Grow these plants in the garden against the base of trees or in rockeries, but shelter them against cold and frost. The woody stems of this plant are slender and brittle, and need staking or some other form of support to keep plants upright. In the colder areas of South Africa, grow these plants in containers with large pine bark chunks but do ensure that they get the brightest light possible, otherwise they will not flower. Water and feed regularly throughout the year. *Vanda* Miss Joaquim flowers throughout the year.

Vanda sanderiana

Vanda sanderiana is a warm-growing epiphyte which is intolerant of temperatures below 10°C. It is not recommended that this species be mounted on trees, even in warmer areas, as cold winds will harm plants. *Vanda sanderiana* is best grown in a container with large pine bark chunks in a warm and sheltered environment where high humidity, with mild air movement, can be provided throughout the year. This species is a robust grower, and must be watered and fed regularly all through the year. The showy flowers appear in autumn to early winter. The hybrids incorporating *Vanda sanderiana* often inherit the large flower size, but are mostly significantly easier to grow in intermediate to warm conditions.

Vanda suavis

Vanda suavis is an intermediate to warm-growing epiphyte. It is closely related to *Vanda luzonica*, and is also sometimes found under the synonym *Vanda tricolor* var. *suavis*. *Vanda suavis* has the same cultural requirements as *Vanda luzonica*, but differs from the latter in that *Vanda suavis* flowers in autumn and winter through to spring, and its flowers are highly scented.

Vanda tricolor

Vanda tricolor is closely related to *Vanda luzonica* and *Vanda suavis*, and has the same cultural requirements. This species flowers in winter to spring and early summer.

Pictures of some Vanda alliance hybrids are on page 110 and 111.

Zygopetalum intermedium (picture on page 112)

Zygopetalum intermedium is an intermediate to cool-growing semi-terrestrial plant which is best grown in containers with a mix of equal parts of medium-sized pine bark chips and commercial potting soil. Plants are robust and grow vigorously, and should be watered and fed copiously throughout the year. This species prefers shading of 40-50%, with high humidity and good air movement. Plants tolerate cold temperatures to 5°C, but should be sheltered from frost. *Zygopetalum intermedium* flowers in spring, and produces 8-12 highly scented 8 centimetres wide flowers on an erect inflorescence. This species and its hybrids are easy to grow and flower.

Vanda suavis

Vanda tricolor

Ascocenda Wacharin - an intergeneric hybrid between *Ascocentrum* and *Vanda*

Ascocenda Chaiyat - a semi-terete hybrid

Ascocenda Yip Sum Wah - a pink form of this popular hybrid

Ascocenda Fuchs Sunkist

Ascocenda John de Biase "Fuchs Indigo"

Vanda Rothschildiana

Vanda Sunset "Perfection"

Ascofinetia Petite Bouquet – an intergeneric miniature hybrid with *Neofinetia falcata*

Zygopetalum intermedium

Zygopetalum Artur Elle

Ascocenda Fuchs Sunkist

6

Repotting and Dividing your Orchids

Orchids are vigorous growers, and when they are grown in pots or other containers, they should be repotted every 2-3 years or earlier if they have outgrown their pots. Plants that are properly positioned with ample room to grow and lots of fresh potting medium at the roots will continue to grow at their full potential, whereas overgrown plants pushing up against the pots, or even outgrowing them may become stunted.

There is a large selection of containers and potting mixes that can be used for orchids, and many growers have good results with a variety of different combinations.

There are a few repotting basics that should be followed religiously if you want to obtain good results. Books from overseas sources often refer to potting mixes such as sphagnum moss, osmunda or tree fern fibre, and a number of unusual additives such as vermiculite or even crushed oak leaves! Most of these items are often not obtainable in South Africa, or if they are, are prohibitively expensive.

In general, the best potting medium for epiphytes is various grades of pine bark, as previously discussed. Always remember to choose the grade of the bark in such a manner as to suit the size of the plant, the size of the pot, as well as the thickness of the roots. Do not overpot your plants - in other words, choose a pot that will accommodate the growths for the next two years at most. If you pot a plant in a container that is far too large for it, you will simply be wasting the potting medium, as the plant cannot use it. An excess of potting medium in a pot also retains too much moisture. This means that the medium will start to degrade prematurely, and it will turn sour or compost-like. It may even cause the roots of the plant to rot, resulting in the death of your precious orchid.

Dendrobium Milky Way "Starlight"

Always put a good amount of crocks in the bottom of the pot. This provides stability to the pot and allows for good drainage. Broken clay pot shards or coarse gravel is best to use. Epiphytic orchid roots require air for their vigorous growth, as one can see by the way they attach themselves to the outside of tree trunks in nature. Plant roots need to be able to dry out somewhat between waterings, so good drainage and the correct grade of bark chunks in the pot will allow air movement through the mix as well, enabling plants to quickly re-establish themselves after they have been repotted.

Different types of containers

Plastic pots

Plastic pots are the cheapest and easiest to obtain, and are easy to clean if you intend to use them again. They come in a wide range of sizes and shapes. Most commercially available plastic pots have only a few small drainage holes in the bottom. For orchids this is not enough. Enlarge the existing holes, or increase their number to ensure good drainage. (The easiest way to enlarge the existing holes is to burn them bigger by means of a small electric soldering iron.) Plastic pots retain moisture for quite a few days, so do check your watering schedule to ensure plants are not kept too wet.

Clay pots

Clay pots are not always easy to obtain, and can be fairly expensive. On account of their porous nature, they are not as hygienic to use as plastic pots as they are difficult to clean if used before. However, clay pots do have the advantage that they allow water to evaporate through their sides. The water evaporating through the pots increases the humidity around the plants, allows the potting medium to dry out faster, and generally tends to keep the roots cool because of the increased evaporation. This enables the grower to cultivate slightly cooler-growing plants in a warmer environment, but does not solve all the problems associated with growing cooler-growing plants in warm areas. Algae sometimes grow on clay pots that are kept too wet. Such algae growth is almost impossible to remove, and reduces the porosity of the pot.

Clay pots do not come in a great variety of sizes, but one can often find a potter to make pots to your specific requirements should you want to. Clay pots are heavier and a little more stable than many other pots, but they break easily when they fall over, especially as they get older and the clay becomes brittle. Plant roots attach themselves very firmly to the rough surface of the pots, and therefore can easily be damaged should you need to repot the plant. It is sometimes even necessary to break a pot in order to remove a plant. Do not use clay pots sealed with a glaze - these pots may be pretty to look at, but do not have any of the benefits of clay pots, as they are no longer porous.

Baskets

Many epiphytic orchids can be grown with great success in baskets. Most garden shops and nurseries stock baskets in various shapes and sizes. The best to use would be baskets made of slats of a hard wood, normally teak. However, wire baskets and even plastic baskets can be used, although plastic baskets tend to become brittle over time, and break. Buy a basket big enough to accommodate the eventual size of the plant, and use medium to large bark chips to anchor the plant in the basket. Place a layer of coir or plastic netting in the bottom to prevent the bark chips from falling out. Plants grown in baskets can be suspended from trees or from patios, and can be positioned to make the best use of the plant's required light and air movement.

Plants in baskets grow well because of the increased air available to the roots. However, because of this very fact the roots often anchor themselves so firmly to the basket that it makes repotting very difficult, as extensive root damage may occur. Therefore, baskets should be made of a material strong enough to last many years, and should allow space for 6-8 years' growth for the plants. The free-draining nature of baskets allows the bark chunks to last longer before they start to break down, which enables the grower to keep the plant in the basket for much longer. Should the plant eventually outgrow the basket and need to be repotted, it may be an option to simply place the entire basket with the plant into a larger one, thus avoiding damage to the plant's roots.

It is not advisable to put seedling plants into baskets. Rather grow a young plant in a pot until it is mature, and only then replant it in a basket if you wish.

General Repotting Guidelines

As a general rule, orchids with a sympodial growth habit such as *Cymbidium*, *Dendrobium* and *Cattleya* should be repotted only after they have finished flowering, and just when the new growths have started appearing. Repotting should be done before the roots on the new growths are too long. This will prevent the new roots from being damaged, and will enable the plant to re-establish itself quickly in its new container.

Orchids with a monopodial growth habit, such as *Vanda* and *Phalaenopsis*, do not, as a rule, produce new growths from the base. They can be repotted at any time, but preferably after flowering, and also at the start of the growing season to allow new roots to establish themselves in the potting medium.

Slipper orchids can be repotted at any time after flowering, but take care not to place these plants too high in the pot. The base of the mature growth must be level with the potting medium, and roots should not be exposed to the air as they will dry out. New growths of slipper orchids also occur at the base of the plant and are very delicate, so take care not to damage them.

When you are repotting your orchids, it is the ideal time to groom your plants as well. Remove any totally dead leaves and canes or pseudobulbs/canes with a sharp blade, knife or scissors. Pseudobulbs or canes at the back of the plant that are soft and mushy must also be cut off, as they are rotting and are no longer of any use to the plant. Canes or pseudobulbs that have lost their leaves, but are still green or firm to the touch should be left on the plant. These still act as a storage mechanism for the plant. It is important to ensure that a cutting instrument is used for only one plant at a time, as viruses and other diseases can be spread to healthy plants when you use contaminated cutting instruments.

Sterilise your cutting instruments between different plants by passing the blades through an open flame, immersing them in a strong bleach solution, or by boiling them in water for ten minutes.

Once you have removed the plant from its pot, wash off all the old potting mix from the roots. If some of the roots are dark-brown in colour and feel soggy and mushy, remove them as well, as they are most probably dead. Orchid roots have a central, wiry stem. If this stem is visible and the surrounding "flesh" of the root has rotted away, the root is dead and must be removed. Live roots should feel firm to the touch, have a creamy-white colour and should have a growing point. Live roots that are exposed to the light will have a green growing point, and will be a pale greyish green in colour. When watered, the roots should be a dark greyish green, as the roots have absorbed the water.

Large plants can now be divided if required. Always leave at least 2-3 leafless back bulbs that are still firm to the touch, and ensure that at least 2 mature growths with leaves also remain per division. A division meeting these criteria will ensure a healthy plant large enough to flower in the next season from the new growth. Make such divisions by cutting through the rhizome at the appropriate point, and seal the cut edge of the rhizome with flowers of sulphur. Should you not wish to divide the plant, it can simply be potted up again after cleaning.

Select a clean or new pot appropriate to the size of the plant (leaving space for no more than 2 years of growth), and fill the bottom third of the pot with crocks. Place the back of the plant at the side of the pot, keeping the growing point in the centre to give it room to grow. Large plants that are kept intact and that have several growing points around the plant, should be placed in the centre of the new pot. Fill the pot with the potting medium, and press down firmly to fill the pot properly and to anchor the plant in the pot. Orchids do not like to be loose in their pots, so be sure to push the medium in firmly. Do not be concerned if one or two roots are damaged in this process, as they will grow again. Leave the plant in a shady area for about a week, and only water lightly during this time. After a week, move the plant to its normal growing area and resume watering and feeding.

The genus *Cymbidium* often has numerous firm leafless back bulbs on large plants. These often occur in the centre of the plant, and in this instance the plant should be divided as these back bulbs will eventually start to decay and may harm the plant. If there are too many leafless back bulbs left on the plant or its divisions, they can be removed. This is done by cutting through the rhizome. Dust the cut edges with flowers of sulphur to seal

Repotting a *Cymbidium*

Recommended *Cymbidium mix* should be loose and friable

Place ample crocks in a clean pot

Overgrown *Cymbidium* before repotting

Root ball, showing brown mushy old roots, with a new whitish root in centre

Trim away dead, mushy roots

Cut away leafless backbulbs

◀ Clean plant by removing dead leaves, bracts and weeds

▼ Newly divided plant ready for repotting. Note new growth and roots at base of mature pseudobulb

Repotting and Dividing your Orchids

Place plant in pot with new growth in the centre. Fill with potting mix

Press down potting mix firmly to anchor the plant

Newly repotted plant. Note the name label which has been put in the pot

Viable leafless backbulb, roots trimmed off. Place in river sand and water regularly to encourage any live eyes to sprout

the wound and to prevent infection. Trim away all the roots and place the single back bulbs upright, about a third deep, in coarse washed river sand. Place in a bright spot and water regularly. If there were any live dormant eyes on such a back bulb, it should sprout, and in time you will have another plant to pot up.

If your plant had a name, label all back bulbs with a name tag, and always ensure that all plants are correctly labelled. This goes for all divisions of plants as well. If a grower ever wishes to dispose of excess plants by selling them, a named plant is worth much more and may sell more easily to other growers who may be looking for a particular species or hybrid, even if it is not in flower. Whereas species orchids can be identified from the flowers, it is not that easy to identify hybrids unless you have another plant in flower to compare it to in order to establish what it is. There are just too many orchid hybrids around for easy identification.

Repotting a Cymbidium

Cymbidiums are some of the easiest orchids to grow, but often do not flower well when they are not repotted properly or regularly. On the previous pages is a photographic guide showing step-by-step how to repot a *Cymbidium*. This process is similar for all epiphytic and semi-terrestrial orchids as described above. Although there are many potting mix suggestions in orchid literature, the following mix is recommended: one part each of washed coarse river sand, medium to large (10-20 mm) pine bark chunks, and one part commercial potting soil. One could even add some polystyrene beads or chips to lighten and aerate the mix, as large plants in big pots can become quite heavy. Polystyrene is inert, does not break down, and does not harm the plants in any way. Do not let the amount of polystyrene exceed a quarter of the mix, as this may make the pots too light and they may be blown over by the wind.

Disa uniflora

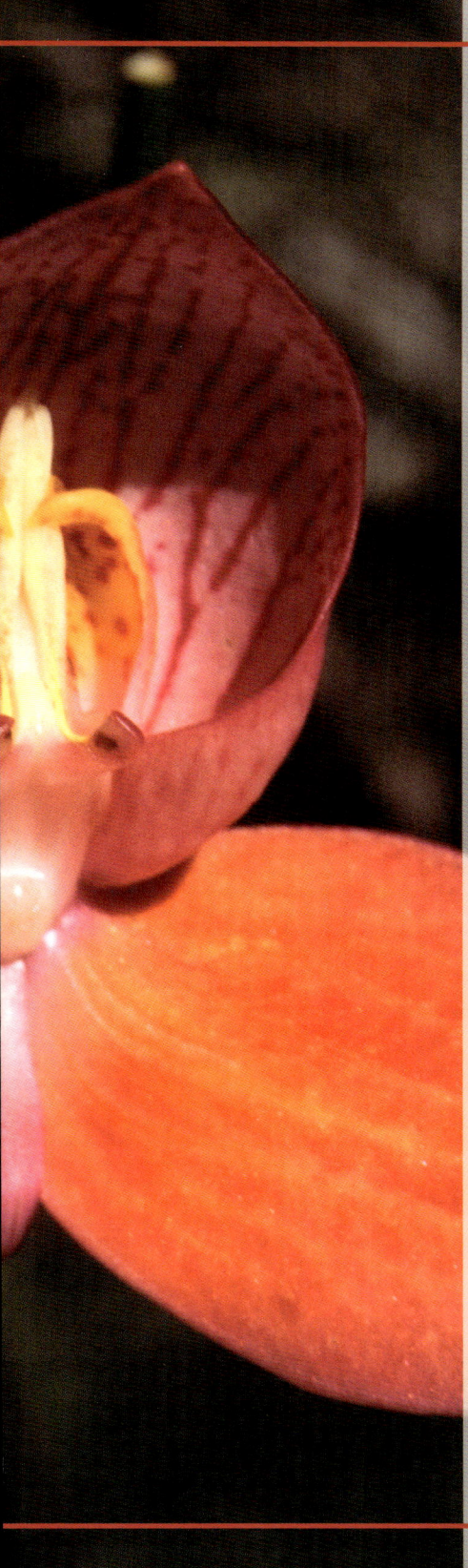

7 Indigenous Orchids

South Africa is known for its floral diversity, and this is also true of its orchids. More than 460 species of orchids call South Africa home, and some truly spectacular orchids are found here. *Disa uniflora* is endemic to the Western Cape, and is grown all over the world, although it is not easy to grow successfully in cultivation.

Orchids in South Africa occur over a wide range of different climates and habitats. Different plants grow from sea level up to high altitudes in the Drakensberg, and are found in all of the provinces. Most of the orchids indigenous to South Africa are plants which grow terrestrially. They are rather difficult to grow in cultivation as they require very strict climatic conditions. In some instances certain orchids will only flower after a veld fire, and others grow only in swampland or in summer or winter rainfall areas. The epiphytes found in South Africa occur mostly in forested areas and are much easier to grow. In fact, most epiphytic species found in the country are grown widely in cultivation, both locally and overseas.

Growers must be aware that all orchid species in South Africa are protected by law, and as such may not be removed from nature without a valid permit. In some instances, possession of certain species may also require a permit. Orchids also appear on the international CITES list specifying endangered plants and animals, and permits are required to move them across international borders, as well as to trade with indigenous species.

Disa cooperi in a field in Himeville, KwaZulu-Natal

There are, however, a number of nurseries which are allowed to sell indigenous orchids which are certified not to have been collected from nature, and which have been grown from seed. Provided you obtain your plants from a reputable source, growers should not have any problems.

The indigenous orchid species, and especially the epiphytes, are normally very easy to grow under intermediate conditions, and these plants do very well mounted on trees in most areas. A number of indigenous species are detailed here for the aspiring grower to obtain and grow. Only a few terrestrial species are mentioned, and these are considered those that the average gardener will be able to maintain in cultivation.

Ansellia africana

Ansellia is a genus of only one species, *Ansellia africana*. This species is found widely throughout southern and tropical Africa, and is immensely variable. The plants that occur in the southernmost part of its range have smaller, clear-yellow flowers. Further north, the flowers increase in size and brown spotting and barring are noticeable on the yellow flowers. At its northernmost occurrence, plants have large yellow (and sometimes even light green) flowers with heavy and intense chocolate-brown markings.

Plants are easy to grow and are very robust, sometimes having canes over 50 centimetres long. The flower spikes are long, also over 50 centimetres, are branched, and carry numerous flowers which appear from early spring to early summer. The flowers often have a pleasing scent.

They are heavy feeders and require ample watering and feeding in the growing season of spring to summer, and only light watering in the cooler winter months when the plant undergoes a resting period. They grow well under intermediate conditions and can tolerate cold, but not frost. Hard, leathery leaves are an indication that this species will tolerate full sunlight throughout the day, although some light shading over midday is recommended. *Ansellia* grows best mounted onto the side of treetrunks where they can get the best light, but can also be grown in pots with large (20 millimetres) chunks of pine bark.

Ansellia africana has two types of root system. It has a normal root system which anchors the plant to the tree on which it is mounted, or which grows in the coarse epiphytic potting mix. The other system has upright, aerial roots. They grow upwards from around the base of the plant and are intended to catch leaves and other detritus falling down from the trees on which they grow. This is called a "trash-basket" system, and the plants utilise their catch for the nutrients contained therein.

Ansellia africana - southernmost form with almost ▲
no brown spotting on flowers

Ansellia africana ▶

Ansellia africana - northernmost form with larger ▼
flowers and dark-brown barring on flowers

Cyrtorchis arcuata

Cyrtorchis arcuata is an easy intermediate grower which does best under shady (50-60 % shade) conditions. It does not tolerate constant cold, but is quite hardy. It does best mounted on a tree or on a slab of bark. It can be grown in a basket with large pine bark chunks, but is not suited to being grown in a pot, as plants can become quite large.

Plants have a woody stem and dark green leaves, and easily form clumps when grown well. Water can be given throughout the year, with no feeding during the cooler winter months. Flowering occurs during mid- to late summer, and the pristine white flowers have a sweet scent, especially at night.

Diaphananthe millarii

Diaphananthe millarii is a shade-loving miniature epiphyte which does best mounted on a slab of bark, or mounted on a tree. It is not suited to container culture. It prefers heavy shade throughout the year, and if grown on a tree must be positioned in such a way that full sunlight is not able to reach and burn the plant.

The species prefers humid, warm environments and must be sheltered from cold and frost. Feed and water regularly throughout the year, as the plant has no storage facility apart from its thick leaves. Flowering occurs in summer.

Diaphananthe xanthopollinia

Diaphananthe xanthopollinia is an intermediate to warm-growing plant which likes dappled shade (40-50%) and humid conditions. It is a rambling grower and is best grown on a tree, mounted on a slab of bark or in a basket with medium (10-20 millimetres) chunks of bark. It should be watered and fed regularly throughout the year as the plant does not have a storage facility other than its short, leathery leaves and woody stems.

This species tolerates occasional temperatures of 5°C, but must be sheltered from frost. The small, diaphanous (translucent) flowers appear from spring until summer.

Disa uniflora

Disa uniflora is probably the most easily recognised South African orchid, and is commonly known as the red disa. It occurs only in very localised areas in the Western Cape, and although it and its related species and hybrids are often seen in literature, this plant cannot be considered easy to grow by any stretch of the imagination. They are very fussy about water quality and nutrient concentration, and must be moist constantly, and may even be grown in running water. Tap water may mean death to these orchids, and it is recommended that people intending to grow them should contact a knowledgeable grower before attempting anything further.

Eulophia speciosa

Eulophia speciosa occurs over a vast area from the southernmost areas of South Africa through to tropical East Africa. The plants can tolerate cold, but not frost. The thick, leathery leaves can withstand full sun throughout the day.

This species can be grown in the garden, however, although it is hardy, it will do better in a slightly sheltered spot. It prefers sandy soil with some compost, and can be grown in a similar medium in large pots. It is a vigorous grower and needs a large container to accommodate it. Water and feed once a week in spring and summer, and only once in 10-14 days in winter as it requires a resting period. Flower stems carry numerous sequentially opening flowers which are quite long-lasting (3-4 weeks) and the stems can be over a metre long. It flowers in spring and summer.

Eulophia streptopetala

Eulophia streptopetala is very similar in its requirements to *Eulophia speciosa* (see above). It differs in that it requires more shade and shelter, as it grows on the edges of forests and grasslands. Protect the plants from cold and frost, and provide 30-40% shade throughout the day. Plants should be watered and fed weekly throughout spring and summer, but stop watering once the leaves turn yellow in autumn to winter. Thereafter, water only once in 3-4 weeks during a warm spell. Resume regular watering and feeding once the new growths start in spring. Plants can be grown in well-drained garden beds

rich in compost, or in suitably large containers with a similar potting medium. Flower stems can be up to one and a half metres long, and appear from early spring onwards.

Liparis remota

Liparis remota is an intermediate-growing miniature terrestrial species. It likes heavy shade (60-70%) throughout the year, and prefers humid and moist conditions. It is a tiny plant with a creeping habit, and can be grown with ease in shallow containers in a mix of one part each of river sand, commercial potting soil and fine compost.

It can be grown in the garden under similar conditions, but must be sheltered from too much sunlight, as well as very low temperatures and frost. As it should be grown in compost-rich soil, it should not need additional feeding, but plants must be watered regularly in spring and summer.

Liparis remota occurs in summer rainfall areas and can be kept somewhat drier in winter, with water given once in 10-14 days only. Flowering occurs during mid- to late summer. *Liparis bowkeri* is very similar in appearance and culture requirements.

Liparis remota

Microcoelia exilis

Microcoelia exilis

Microcoelia exilis is an unusual plant in that it is totally leafless when mature. Plants only have leaves when they are very young. The roots of this species contain chloroplasts to perform photosynthesis, and must be exposed to light in order to do this. As such, this species can only be grown mounted or on a tree under conditions of 30-40 % shade.

It likes intermediate humid conditions and should be watered and fed regularly throughout the year. Healthy, live roots will appear dark-green when wet. The plants grow vigorously and form large clumps. The very tiny flowers appear in spring.

Mystacidium brayboniae

Mystacidium brayboniae is an intermediate to warm-growing miniature epiphytic plant. It does best when mounted on a small dead branch or a slab of bark, and is not suited to being grown in a container. It can be mounted on a tree. The plants like humid conditions with dappled to heavy shade (50-60 %) throughout the year. This species cannot tolerate frost and cold temperatures.

Mystacidium brayboniae has very short, leathery leaves, and may lose its leaves in the dry season (winter). To avoid this, it should be watered throughout the year. Water twice weekly in spring and summer, and once in 7-10 days in winter. Feeding can be given in spring and summer. The flowering time is spring to early summer.

Mystacidium capense

Mystacidium capense is an intermediate-growing miniature plant which prefers dappled shade (50%) and humid conditions. It can withstand low temperatures for short periods (not below 5°C), but must be sheltered from frost.

This species is best grown mounted on a tree, piece of bark or a dead branch. It is not suited to being grown in a container. Like most South African epiphytes, it has a rambling root system which does not like being confined. The plant has no storage facility and must be watered and fed regularly throughout the year, with heavy watering in spring and summer. The sweet-scented, white flowers occur in summer.

Mystacidium venosum

Mystacidium venosum is similar to *Mystacidium capense* (above) in all cultural requirements, and even its appearance. The main difference is that *Mystacidium venosum* flowers in winter.

Mystacidium brayboniae ▲
Mystacidium capense ▶
Mystacidium venosum ▼

Polystachya pubescens

Polystachya ottoniana

Polystachya ottoniana is a charming miniature epiphyte which occurs in a wide range of colours, including white, yellow, green, pink and brown. It has a creeping habit and the small, round pseudobulbs, each with 2-3 deciduous leaves, form dense mats on branches or bark mounts. Plants grow under intermediate conditions, and like ample watering and feeding during spring and summer. Water only once in 10 days in winter to avoid excessive shrivelling of the pseudobulbs.

Provide 30% shade throughout the year. *Polystachya ottoniana* is a hardy plant which will tolerate temperatures down to 2°C, but it must be sheltered from frost. Plants may lose their leaves during winter, and flower in spring from the new growths.

Polystachya pubescens

Polystachya pubescens is an intermediate-growing plant which likes bright light and good humidity throughout the year. It can be mounted, or grown in a container with medium 10-15 millimetres pine bark chunks. It will tolerate full sunlight, but should preferably receive some shade during the hottest time of day. In nature this species sometimes occurs lithophytically.

Water regularly (2-3 times a week) and feed once a week during spring and summer. This species requires a rest period in winter and should only be watered once in 7-10 days to avoid excessive shrivelling of the pseudobulbs. Flowers appear in spring and open successively over several weeks.

Polystachya ottoniana - yellow form growing on a tree

Polystachya ottoniana - white form growing on a slab of bark

Indigenous Orchids

Sophrolaeliocattleya Coastal Sunrise "Pink Surprise"

Contact Information

Paphiopedilum insigne as a garden plant under shady trees at Makaranga Lodge, Kloof

There are several orchid societies in South Africa which are affiliated to the South African Orchid Council (SAOC). These societies hold regular monthly meetings where members bring their plants in flower to show on the plant table. A knowledgeable member or an accredited judge of the SAOC will discuss the plants brought in for display. Speakers are also often invited to present talks on a specific topic related to the growing or breeding of orchids.

Many societies hold an annual show to show off plants in flower to the general public, and ribbons and trophies are presented to the best plants in each category. Plant sales are normally held at these shows. SAOC awards may also be granted to plants of sufficient quality and merit. The SAOC holds a national show every three years. This national show rotates to various areas around the country, and is always held in conjunction with a symposium on orchids.

At such a symposium, various local and international speakers are invited to present talks on a large range of subjects related to orchids, and plants are also offered for sale by many local and international growers and nurseries. Contact your local orchid society or the SAOC for more information on meetings and show venues. Members of the SAOC receive a full-colour yearbook containing numerous articles on orchids, as well as regular newsletters providing information on shows and other events to be held.

Contact details

South African Orchid Council - P O Box 85, Edenvale, 1610

E-mail : mikeandtessa@mweb.co.za

Web site: www.saoc.co.za

Cape Orchid Society - P O Box 3347, Cape Town, 8000 (Cape Town)

Eastern Province Orchid Society - P O Box 28678, Sunridge Park, Port Elizabeth, 6008

Free State Orchid Society - P O Box 13968, Noordstad, 9302 (Bloemfontein)

Gonubie Orchid Society - P O Box 179, Gonubie, 5256 (East London)

Lowveld Orchid Group - P O Box 1917, Nelspruit, 1200

Natal Orchid Society - P O Box 47275, Greyville, 4023 (Durban)

Orchid Society of the N Transvaal - P O Box 34900, Glenstantia, 0010 (Pretoria)

Pietermaritzburg Orchid Society - P O Box 862, Pietermaritzburg, 3200

Queensburgh Orchid Club - P O Box 1545, Kloof, 3640 (Durban surrounds)

Tygerberg Orchid Group - P O Box 195, Belville, 7530 (Cape Town surrounds)

Umhlatuzana Orchid Species Society - P O Box 939, Gillitts, 3603
(Durban surrounds, specialist group for species orchids)

Witwatersrand Orchid Society - P O Box 72007, Parkview, 2122 (Johannesburg)

Wolkberg Orchid Society - P O Box 47, Tzaneen, 0850 (Tzaneen and surrounds)

Zululand Orchid Society - P O Box 10044, Empangeni, 3880 (Empangeni and surrounds)

The author, Hendrik Venter : e-mail hendrik2@mweb.co.za

Cymbidium Bulbarrow

Recommended Further Reading

References

Index

Recommended Further Reading

"Only some orchid growers are beginners, but all orchid growers are learners" (Hugh Rogers circa 1990).

Those readers that may want to learn a bit more can try to get hold of some of the books mentioned below.

Bechtel, H., Cribb, P. & Launert, E. 1992. *Manual of Cultivated Orchid Species*. 3rd edition. Trade Winds Press (Pty) Ltd., South Africa.

Fanfani, A. 1988. The *MacDonald Encyclopaedia of Orchids*. MacDonald & Co.(Publishers) Ltd., Great Britain.

Hawkes, A.D. 1965. *Encyclopaedia of Cultivated Orchids*. Faber and Faber, London.

Holliman, J. (ed.) 2002. *Botanica's Pocket Orchids*. Random House, Australia.

Jeźek, Z. 2003. *The Complete Encyclopaedia of Orchids*. Rebo International, Netherlands.

Pridgeon, A. 1992. *What Orchid is That?* Weldon Publishing, Sydney, Australia.

Rentoul, J.N. 1980- *Growing Orchids* (various volumes). Lothian Publishing, Australia.

South African Orchid Council-Journals and Yearbooks. 1978-2004. Numerous articles and authors.

Stewart, J., Linder, H.P., Schelpe, E.A. & Hall, A. 1982. *Wild Orchids of Southern Africa*. MacMillan, Johannesburg.

Wodrich, K.H.K. 1997. *Growing South African Indigenous Orchids*. A.A. Balkema, Rotterdam, Netherlands.

Author's note: Some of these recommended titles may no longer be available in the trade. Local orchid societies have libraries which their members may use, and most of the titles will be in these libraries. Orchid society libraries may also have back copies of the SAOC journal for members to peruse.

Orchid books can be obtained online from: www.kalahari.net , www.amazon.com , and www.aos.org . Many bookstores will also be able to assist readers in obtaining orchid books that may be available, even though not in-store.

References

Bechtel, H., Cribb, P. & Launert, E. 1992. *Manual of Cultivated Orchid Species*. 3rd edition, Trade Winds Press (Pty) Ltd., South Africa.

Fanfani, A. 1988. *The MacDonald Encyclopaedia of Orchids*. MacDonald & Co.(Publishers) Ltd., Great Britain.

Holliman, J. (ed.) 2002. *Botanica's Pocket Orchids*. Random House, Australia.

Jeźek, Z. 2003. *The Complete Encyclopaedia of Orchids*. Rebo International, Netherlands.

Pridgeon, A. 1992. *What Orchid is That?* Weldon Publishing, Sydney, Australia.

South African Orchid Council-Journals and Yearbooks. 1978-2004. Numerous articles and authors.

Wodrich, K.H.K. 1997. *Growing South African Indigenous Orchids*. A.A. Balkema, Rotterdam, Netherlands.

Index

Page numbers in bold indicate illustrations.

A
Air movement 31
Aerangis stylosa 52, **52**
Angraecum eburneum 31
Angraecum leonis 52, **52**
Angraecum sesquipedale 52, **52**
Angraecum superbum 31
Ansellia Africana 127, **127**
Arachnis flos-aeris 52
Arachnis Maggie-Oei 53, **53**
Arum lilies 31
Arundina graminifolia 27, 53, **53**
Ascocenda Chaiyat **110**
Ascocenda Fuchs Sunkist **110**, **114**
Ascocenda John de Biase "Fuchs Indigo" **111**
Ascocenda Wacharin **110**
Ascocenda Yip Sum Wah **110**
Ascocentrum ampullaceum 53, **53**
Ascocentrum ampullaceum var. *album* 53, **54**
Ascocentrum curvifolium 53, **54**
Ascocentrum miniatum 53, **54**
Ascofinetia Petite Bouquet **111**

B
Bifrenaria harrisoniae **55**, 55
Bifrenaria harrisoniae var. *alba* 54
Bletilla striata 55, **55**
Bletilla striata 54
Brassavola cucullata 55, **55**
Brassavola nodosa 56, **56**
Brassia verrucosa 56, **56**
Brassolaeliocattleya Alma Kee "Tip Malee" **63**
Brassolaeliocattleya Chunyeah **63**
Brassolaeliocattleya Nacouchee "Mission Valley" **63**
Bulbophyllum species 24

C
Calanthe Saint Aubin **57**
Calanthe (Saint Aubin x Diana Broughton) **57**
Calanthe Sedenii Harrisii **57**
Calanthe vestita 56, **56**
Calanthe victoria-regina 57, **57**
Cattley, William 8
Cattleya - sympodial growth habit **18**

Cattleya amethystoglossa 58, **58**
Cattleya aurantiaca **32**, 58, **58**
Cattleya bicolor 58, **58**
Cattleya Clark Herman "Carl" **63**
Cattleya flower **15**
Cattleya forbesii 59, **59**
Cattleya gaskelliana 59, **59**
Cattleya harrisoniana 61, **61**
Cattleya Horace "Maxima" **82**
Cattleya intermedia 59, **59**
Cattleya intermedia var. *orlata* **60**
Cattleya labiata 8, 9, 60, **60**
Cattleya loddigesii **60**, 61
Cattleya luteola 61, **61**
Cattleya maxima 61, **61**
Cattleya warneri 64, **64**
Coelogyne cristata 64, **64**
Coelogyne cristata var. *hololeuca* **64**
Coelogyne flaccida 64, **65**
Contact information 136-137
Containers for potting orchids 117
Cuitlauzina pendula 65, **65**
Cymbidium - sympodial growth habit **18**
Cymbidium Bulbarrow 67, **138**
Cymbidium erythrostylum 65, **65**
Cymbidium Fancy Free "Geyserland" **68**
Cymbidium flower **15**
Cymbidium lowianum 66, **66**
Cymbidium lowianum var. *concolor* 66, **66**
Cymbidium Nicole's Valentine 67
Cymbidium Oakbank **12**, **68**
Cymbidium Rocky Creek "Tregarthen" **14**
Cymbidium Seagem "Wildroot" **39**
Cymbidium Strathbraan "Cooksbridge Noel" **68**
Cymbidium Strathcoil "Oudepost Princess" **68**
Cymbidium Tommy 67
Cymbidium Winter Fire "Faultless" **67**
Cyrtorchis arcuata 128, **128**

D
Dendrobium - sympodial growth habit **18**
Dendrobium (Lady Pink x Classic Gem) **70**
Dendrobium bigibbum 42, 69

Dendrobium bigibbum var. *compactum* **69**
Dendrobium chrysotoxum 69, **69**
Dendrobium densiflorum 71, **71**
Dendrobium fimbriatum var. *oculatum* 71, **71**
Dendrobium flower **15**
Dendrobium Gillieston Jazz **72**
Dendrobium Jesmond Glitter **72**
Dendrobium June Mac **42**
Dendrobium King Dragon **70**
Dendrobium kingianum 71, **71**, 73, **73**
Dendrobium Mild Yumi "Dream" **6**
Dendrobium Milky Way "Starlight" **116**
Dendrobium moschatum 73, **73**
Dendrobium Mousmee "Colleen" **title page**
Dendrobium Nida "Rage" **70**
Dendrobium nobile **40**, 74, **74**
Dendrobium nobile var. *virginale* 74, **74**
Dendrobium Orange Gem **75**
Dendrobium Pittero Gold "Grace" **75**
Dendrobium Pravith White **41**
Dendrobium Prima Donna **75**
Dendrobium Rutherford's Blushing Bride **72**
Dendrobium Sakura "Hine" **75**
Dendrobium speciosum 76, **76**
Dendrobium tetragonum 76, **76**
Dendrobium Thailand **70**
Dendrobium thyrsiflorum 77, **77**
Dendrobium Yondi Gold **72**
Diaphananthe millarii 128, **128**
Diaphananthe xanthopollinia 128, **128**
Disa cooperi **126**
Disa graminifolia **14**
Disa uniflora **27**, **125**, 129, **129**
Dividing orchids 115

E
Encyclia fragrans 77, **77**
Encyclia prismatocarpa 77, **77**
Epidendrum radicans 78, **78**
Epidendrum secundum 78, **78**
Epilaeliocattleya Don Herman "Gold Rush" **62**
Epiphytic orchids growing on a tree **25**, **28**
Eulophia angolensis **29**
Eulophia speciosa 129, **129**
Eulophia streptopetala 129, **129**

F
Feeding orchids 33
Flower structure 15
Flowering habits 19

G
Giant's Castle, South Africa 8
Glossary of terms 19
Goodyera daibuzanensis 78, **78**
Growth medium 25
Growth types 17

H
Hormidium prismatocarpum 77, **77**
Humidity 28

I
Indigenous orchids 125

L
Laelia anceps **33**, 79, **79**
Laelia anceps var. *veitchiana* 79, 79
Laelia crispa 79, **79**
Laelia flava 80, **80**
Laelia lundii 80, **80**
Laelia milleri 80, **80**
Laelia purpurata 81, **81**
Laelia purpurata var. *werckhauser* 81, **81**
Laeliocattleya Canhamiana **10**
Laeliocattleya Gold Digger "Buttercup" **82**
Laeliocattleya Irene Holguin **38**
Laeliocattleya Mini Purple "Lea" **62**
Laeliocattleya Nora's Melody **20**
Laeliocattleya Puppy Love "True Beauty" **62**
Light 29
Liparis remota 130, **130**
Ludisia discolor 83, **83**

M
Maclellanara Pagan Love Song "Ruby Charles" **87**
Masdevallia 10
Maxillaria picta 83, **83**
Maxillaria variabilis 84, **84**
Microcoelia exilis 130, **130**
Miltassia Explorer **86**

Miltonia clowesii 84, **84**
Miltonia flavescens 84, **84**
Miltonia flower **15**
Miltonia moreliana 85, **85**
Miltonia regnellii 85, **85**
Miltonia spectabilis 85, **85**
Miltonia spectabilis "Abigail" **35**
Miltonia spectabilis var. *alba* 85, **86**
Miltonia spectabilis var. *roseum* 85, **86**
Miltonia x *bluntii* **48**
Mystacidium brayboniae 131, **131**
Mystacidium capense 131, **131**
Mystacidium venosum 131, **131**

N
Neofinetia falcata 88, **88**

O
Odontocidium Artur Elle **91**
Oncidium flexuosum 88, **88**
Oncidium Gower Ramsey "Volcano Queen" **91**
Oncidium Nancy **91**
Oncidium ornithorhynchum 89, **89**
Oncidium sarcodes 89, **89**
Oncidium Sharry Baby "Sweet Fragrance" **91**
Oncidium sphacelatum 24, 26, 49, 90, **90**

P
Paphiopedilum Armeni White **96**
Paphiopedilum British Bulldog "Rage" **97**
Paphiopedilum callosum 92, **92**
Paphiopedilum Carmen Coll **97**
Paphiopedilum concolor 92, **92**
Paphiopedilum delenatii 92, **92**
Paphiopedilum flower **16**
Paphiopedilum hirsutissimum 93, **93**
Paphiopedilum Inca "Robe" **97**
Paphiopedilum insigne 22, 28, 93, **93**, **136**
Paphiopedilum Leeanum **43**
Paphiopedilum Macabre **96**
Paphiopedilum Maudiae **44**
Paphiopedilum Maudiae "The Queen" **96**
Paphiopedilum micranthum **94**
Paphiopedilum micranthum "Christian" **94**
Paphiopedilum parishii **94**
Paphiopedilum parishii "Wiaan" **94**

Paphiopedilum rothschildianum **11**
Paphiopedilum sukhakulii 95, **95**
Paphiopedilum Tommie Hanes "Williamdale" **97**
Paphiopedilum villosum 95, **95**
Paphiopedilum Vintner's Treasure "Rage" **96**
Pests and diseases **34**
Phaius tankervilleae 30, 103, **103**
Phaius tankervilleae var. *alba* 103, **103**
Phalaenopsis Pink Leopard "Petra"
 French title page
Phalaenopsis amabilis 36, 98, **98**
Phalaenopsis Bonnie Vasquez
 "Zuma Canyon" **102**
Phalaenopsis Brother Pico Chip **45**
Phalaenopsis Dou-dii Girl **101**
Phalaenopsis equestris 98, **98**
Phalaenopsis Ever-spring King **101**
Phalaenopsis Flor de Niebla 50, **100**
Phalaenopsis flower **16**
Phalaenopsis Hatsuyuki **102**
Phalaenopsis hybrid **31**
Phalaenopsis Judy Freed **102**
Phalaenopsis lindenii 100, **101**
Phalaenopsis lueddemanniana 98, **99**
Phalaenopsis Michael Tibbs **100**
Phalaenopsis Red Thrill **101**
Phalaenopsis schilleriana 98, **99**
Phalaenopsis stuartiana 98, **99**
Phalaenopsis Taipei Gold **102**
Phalaenopsis violacea 98, **99**
Polystachya ottoniana 133, **133**
Polystachya pubescens 132, **133**
Potinara Little Toshie "Gold Country" **82**
Prosthechea prismatocarpa 77, **77**

R
Renanthera imschootiana 104, **104**
Renanthera monachica 104, **104**
Repotting orchids 115-123
Rhizanthella **11**

S
Sander **8**
Schomburgkia tibicinis 104, **104**
Sobralia macrantha 105, **105**

Sophrolaeliocattleya Bright Angel **62**
Sophrolaeliocattleya Coastal Sunrise
   "Pink Surprise" **82**, **134**
Stanhopea connata 105, **105**
Stanhopea oculata 105, **105**
Stanhopea wardii **26**, 105, **106**
Swanson, William 8

T
Temperature 31

V
Vanda - monopodial growth habit **17**
Vanda Carmen Coll **47**
Vanda coerulea 107, **107**
Vanda flower 16
Vanda luzonica 108, **108**
Vanda Miss Joaquim **34**, **46**, 108, **108**
Vanda Nellie Morley **47**
Vanda Rothschildiana **111**
Vanda sanderiana 108, **108**
Vanda suavis 109, **109**
Vanda Sunset "Perfection" **111**
Vanda tricolor 109, **109**
Veitch 8
Vuylstekeara Violet Wood **86**

W
Watering 26

Z
Zygopetalum Artur Elle **113**
Zygopetalum intermedium 109, **112**

Photo Credits

Cattleya labiata - Carmen Coll - page 9
Vanda Carmen Coll - Carmen Coll - page 47
Oncidium sphacelatum - Hendrelien Peters - page 49
Arachnis Maggie-Oei - Carmen Coll - page 53
Brassavola nodosa - Carmen Coll - page 56
Cattleya harrisoniae - Carmen Coll - page 61
Cymbidium Oakbank - Carmen Coll - page 12, 68
Dendrobium (Lady Pink x Classic Gem) - Hendrelien Peters - page 70
Dendrobium Rutherford's Blushing Bride - Endre Bakro - page 72
Dendrobium Jesmond Glitter - Endre Bakro - page 72
Dendrobium Yondi Gold - Endre Bakro - page 72
Dendrobium Gillieston Jazz - Endre Bakro - page 72
Dendrobium tetragonum - Endre Bakro - page 76
Laelia anceps - Hugh Rogers - page 79
Paphiopedilum Vintner's Treasure "Rage" - Carmen Coll - page 96
Paphiopedilum Tommie Hanes "Williamdale" - Carmen Coll - page 97
Paphiopedilum British Bulldog "Rage" - Carmen Coll - page 97
Paphiopedilum Carmen Coll - Carmen Coll - page 97
Phalaenopsis violacea - Carmen Coll - page 99
Stanhopea connata - Carmen Coll - page 105
Vanda coerulea - Hendrelien Peters - page 107
Vanda luzonica - Carmen Coll - page 108

All other photos by Hendrik Venter